C-3340   CAREER EXAMINATION SERIES

This is your
PASSBOOK for...

Supply Clerk

Test Preparation Study Guide
Questions & Answers

NATIONAL LEARNING CORPORATION®

COPYRIGHT NOTICE

This book is SOLELY intended for, is sold ONLY to, and its use is RESTRICTED to individual, bona fide applicants or candidates who qualify by virtue of having seriously filed applications for appropriate license, certificate, professional and/or promotional advancement, higher school matriculation, scholarship, or other legitimate requirements of education and/or governmental authorities.

This book is NOT intended for use, class instruction, tutoring, training, duplication, copying, reprinting, excerption, or adaptation, etc., by:

1) Other publishers
2) Proprietors and/or Instructors of "Coaching" and/or Preparatory Courses
3) Personnel and/or Training Divisions of commercial, industrial, and governmental organizations
4) Schools, colleges, or universities and/or their departments and staffs, including teachers and other personnel
5) Testing Agencies or Bureaus
6) Study groups which seek by the purchase of a single volume to copy and/or duplicate and/or adapt this material for use by the group as a whole without having purchased individual volumes for each of the members of the group
7) Et al.

Such persons would be in violation of appropriate Federal and State statutes.

PROVISION OF LICENSING AGREEMENTS – Recognized educational, commercial, industrial, and governmental institutions and organizations, and others legitimately engaged in educational pursuits, including training, testing, and measurement activities, may address request for a licensing agreement to the copyright owners, who will determine whether, and under what conditions, including fees and charges, the materials in this book may be used them. In other words, a licensing facility exists for the legitimate use of the material in this book on other than an individual basis. However, it is asseverated and affirmed here that the material in this book CANNOT be used without the receipt of the express permission of such a licensing agreement from the Publishers. Inquiries re licensing should be addressed to the company, attention rights and permissions department.

All rights reserved, including the right of reproduction in whole or in part, in any form or by any means, electronic or mechanical, including photocopying, recording, or by any information storage and retrieval system, without permission in writing from the Publisher.

Copyright © 2025 by
National Learning Corporation

212 Michael Drive, Syosset, NY 11791
(516) 921-8888 • www.passbooks.com
E-mail: info@passbooks.com

PASSBOOK® SERIES

THE *PASSBOOK® SERIES* has been created to prepare applicants and candidates for the ultimate academic battlefield – the examination room.

At some time in our lives, each and every one of us may be required to take an examination – for validation, matriculation, admission, qualification, registration, certification, or licensure.

Based on the assumption that every applicant or candidate has met the basic formal educational standards, has taken the required number of courses, and read the necessary texts, the *PASSBOOK® SERIES* furnishes the one special preparation which may assure passing with confidence, instead of failing with insecurity. Examination questions – together with answers – are furnished as the basic vehicle for study so that the mysteries of the examination and its compounding difficulties may be eliminated or diminished by a sure method.

This book is meant to help you pass your examination provided that you qualify and are serious in your objective.

The entire field is reviewed through the huge store of content information which is succinctly presented through a provocative and challenging approach – the question-and-answer method.

A climate of success is established by furnishing the correct answers at the end of each test.

You soon learn to recognize types of questions, forms of questions, and patterns of questioning. You may even begin to anticipate expected outcomes.

You perceive that many questions are repeated or adapted so that you can gain acute insights, which may enable you to score many sure points.

You learn how to confront new questions, or types of questions, and to attack them confidently and work out the correct answers.

You note objectives and emphases, and recognize pitfalls and dangers, so that you may make positive educational adjustments.

Moreover, you are kept fully informed in relation to new concepts, methods, practices, and directions in the field.

You discover that you are actually taking the examination all the time: you are preparing for the examination by "taking" an examination, not by reading extraneous and/or supererogatory textbooks.

In short, this PASSBOOK®, used directedly, should be an important factor in helping you to pass your test.

SUPPLY CLERK

DUTIES
These positions involve receiving, unloading, storing and distributing various items such as clothing, mail, tools, machine parts, material and supplies, etc., depending on the location and title of the position. Accurate records must be kept of material handled. Performs related duties.

SCOPE OF THE EXAMINATION
The written test will be designed to test for knowledge, skills, and/or abilities in such areas as:
1. Keeping simple inventory records;
2. Organizing data into tables and records;
3. Name and number checking; and
4. Arithmetic computation.

HOW TO TAKE A TEST

I. YOU MUST PASS AN EXAMINATION

A. *WHAT EVERY CANDIDATE SHOULD KNOW*

Examination applicants often ask us for help in preparing for the written test. What can I study in advance? What kinds of questions will be asked? How will the test be given? How will the papers be graded?

As an applicant for a civil service examination, you may be wondering about some of these things. Our purpose here is to suggest effective methods of advance study and to describe civil service examinations.

Your chances for success on this examination can be increased if you know how to prepare. Those "pre-examination jitters" can be reduced if you know what to expect. You can even experience an adventure in good citizenship if you know why civil service exams are given.

B. *WHY ARE CIVIL SERVICE EXAMINATIONS GIVEN?*

Civil service examinations are important to you in two ways. As a citizen, you want public jobs filled by employees who know how to do their work. As a job seeker, you want a fair chance to compete for that job on an equal footing with other candidates. The best-known means of accomplishing this two-fold goal is the competitive examination.

Exams are widely publicized throughout the nation. They may be administered for jobs in federal, state, city, municipal, town or village governments or agencies.

Any citizen may apply, with some limitations, such as the age or residence of applicants. Your experience and education may be reviewed to see whether you meet the requirements for the particular examination. When these requirements exist, they are reasonable and applied consistently to all applicants. Thus, a competitive examination may cause you some uneasiness now, but it is your privilege and safeguard.

C. *HOW ARE CIVIL SERVICE EXAMS DEVELOPED?*

Examinations are carefully written by trained technicians who are specialists in the field known as "psychological measurement," in consultation with recognized authorities in the field of work that the test will cover. These experts recommend the subject matter areas or skills to be tested; only those knowledges or skills important to your success on the job are included. The most reliable books and source materials available are used as references. Together, the experts and technicians judge the difficulty level of the questions.

Test technicians know how to phrase questions so that the problem is clearly stated. Their ethics do not permit "trick" or "catch" questions. Questions may have been tried out on sample groups, or subjected to statistical analysis, to determine their usefulness.

Written tests are often used in combination with performance tests, ratings of training and experience, and oral interviews. All of these measures combine to form the best-known means of finding the right person for the right job.

II. HOW TO PASS THE WRITTEN TEST

A. NATURE OF THE EXAMINATION

To prepare intelligently for civil service examinations, you should know how they differ from school examinations you have taken. In school you were assigned certain definite pages to read or subjects to cover. The examination questions were quite detailed and usually emphasized memory. Civil service exams, on the other hand, try to discover your present ability to perform the duties of a position, plus your potentiality to learn these duties. In other words, a civil service exam attempts to predict how successful you will be. Questions cover such a broad area that they cannot be as minute and detailed as school exam questions.

In the public service similar kinds of work, or positions, are grouped together in one "class." This process is known as *position-classification*. All the positions in a class are paid according to the salary range for that class. One class title covers all of these positions, and they are all tested by the same examination.

B. FOUR BASIC STEPS

1) Study the announcement

How, then, can you know what subjects to study? Our best answer is: "Learn as much as possible about the class of positions for which you've applied." The exam will test the knowledge, skills and abilities needed to do the work.

Your most valuable source of information about the position you want is the official exam announcement. This announcement lists the training and experience qualifications. Check these standards and apply only if you come reasonably close to meeting them.

The brief description of the position in the examination announcement offers some clues to the subjects which will be tested. Think about the job itself. Review the duties in your mind. Can you perform them, or are there some in which you are rusty? Fill in the blank spots in your preparation.

Many jurisdictions preview the written test in the exam announcement by including a section called "Knowledge and Abilities Required," "Scope of the Examination," or some similar heading. Here you will find out specifically what fields will be tested.

2) Review your own background

Once you learn in general what the position is all about, and what you need to know to do the work, ask yourself which subjects you already know fairly well and which need improvement. You may wonder whether to concentrate on improving your strong areas or on building some background in your fields of weakness. When the announcement has specified "some knowledge" or "considerable knowledge," or has used adjectives like "beginning principles of…" or "advanced … methods," you can get a clue as to the number and difficulty of questions to be asked in any given field. More questions, and hence broader coverage, would be included for those subjects which are more important in the work. Now weigh your strengths and weaknesses against the job requirements and prepare accordingly.

3) Determine the level of the position

Another way to tell how intensively you should prepare is to understand the level of the job for which you are applying. Is it the entering level? In other words, is this the position in which beginners in a field of work are hired? Or is it an intermediate or advanced level? Sometimes this is indicated by such words as "Junior" or "Senior" in the class title. Other jurisdictions use Roman numerals to designate the level – Clerk I, Clerk II, for example. The word "Supervisor" sometimes appears in the title. If the level is not indicated by the title, check the description of duties. Will you be working under very close supervision, or will you have responsibility for independent decisions in this work?

4) Choose appropriate study materials

Now that you know the subjects to be examined and the relative amount of each subject to be covered, you can choose suitable study materials. For beginning level jobs, or even advanced ones, if you have a pronounced weakness in some aspect of your training, read a modern, standard textbook in that field. Be sure it is up to date and has general coverage. Such books are normally available at your library, and the librarian will be glad to help you locate one. For entry-level positions, questions of appropriate difficulty are chosen – neither highly advanced questions, nor those too simple. Such questions require careful thought but not advanced training.

If the position for which you are applying is technical or advanced, you will read more advanced, specialized material. If you are already familiar with the basic principles of your field, elementary textbooks would waste your time. Concentrate on advanced textbooks and technical periodicals. Think through the concepts and review difficult problems in your field.

These are all general sources. You can get more ideas on your own initiative, following these leads. For example, training manuals and publications of the government agency which employs workers in your field can be useful, particularly for technical and professional positions. A letter or visit to the government department involved may result in more specific study suggestions, and certainly will provide you with a more definite idea of the exact nature of the position you are seeking.

III. KINDS OF TESTS

Tests are used for purposes other than measuring knowledge and ability to perform specified duties. For some positions, it is equally important to test ability to make adjustments to new situations or to profit from training. In others, basic mental abilities not dependent on information are essential. Questions which test these things may not appear as pertinent to the duties of the position as those which test for knowledge and information. Yet they are often highly important parts of a fair examination. For very general questions, it is almost impossible to help you direct your study efforts. What we can do is to point out some of the more common of these general abilities needed in public service positions and describe some typical questions.

1) General information

Broad, general information has been found useful for predicting job success in some kinds of work. This is tested in a variety of ways, from vocabulary lists to questions about current events. Basic background in some field of work, such as sociology or economics, may be sampled in a group of questions. Often these are principles which have become familiar to most persons through exposure rather than through formal training. It is difficult to advise you how to study for these questions; being alert to the world around you is our best suggestion.

2) Verbal ability

An example of an ability needed in many positions is verbal or language ability. Verbal ability is, in brief, the ability to use and understand words. Vocabulary and grammar tests are typical measures of this ability. Reading comprehension or paragraph interpretation questions are common in many kinds of civil service tests. You are given a paragraph of written material and asked to find its central meaning.

3) Numerical ability

Number skills can be tested by the familiar arithmetic problem, by checking paired lists of numbers to see which are alike and which are different, or by interpreting charts and graphs. In the latter test, a graph may be printed in the test booklet which you are asked to use as the basis for answering questions.

4) Observation

A popular test for law-enforcement positions is the observation test. A picture is shown to you for several minutes, then taken away. Questions about the picture test your ability to observe both details and larger elements.

5) Following directions

In many positions in the public service, the employee must be able to carry out written instructions dependably and accurately. You may be given a chart with several columns, each column listing a variety of information. The questions require you to carry out directions involving the information given in the chart.

6) Skills and aptitudes

Performance tests effectively measure some manual skills and aptitudes. When the skill is one in which you are trained, such as typing or shorthand, you can practice. These tests are often very much like those given in business school or high school courses. For many of the other skills and aptitudes, however, no short-time preparation can be made. Skills and abilities natural to you or that you have developed throughout your lifetime are being tested.

Many of the general questions just described provide all the data needed to answer the questions and ask you to use your reasoning ability to find the answers. Your best preparation for these tests, as well as for tests of facts and ideas, is to be at your physical and mental best. You, no doubt, have your own methods of getting into an exam-taking mood and keeping "in shape." The next section lists some ideas on this subject.

IV. KINDS OF QUESTIONS

Only rarely is the "essay" question, which you answer in narrative form, used in civil service tests. Civil service tests are usually of the short-answer type. Full instructions for answering these questions will be given to you at the examination. But in case this is your first experience with short-answer questions and separate answer sheets, here is what you need to know:

1) Multiple-choice Questions

Most popular of the short-answer questions is the "multiple choice" or "best answer" question. It can be used, for example, to test for factual knowledge, ability to solve problems or judgment in meeting situations found at work.

A multiple-choice question is normally one of three types—
- It can begin with an incomplete statement followed by several possible endings. You are to find the one ending which *best* completes the statement, although some of the others may not be entirely wrong.
- It can also be a complete statement in the form of a question which is answered by choosing one of the statements listed.

- It can be in the form of a problem – again you select the best answer.

Here is an example of a multiple-choice question with a discussion which should give you some clues as to the method for choosing the right answer:

When an employee has a complaint about his assignment, the action which will *best* help him overcome his difficulty is to
- A. discuss his difficulty with his coworkers
- B. take the problem to the head of the organization
- C. take the problem to the person who gave him the assignment
- D. say nothing to anyone about his complaint

In answering this question, you should study each of the choices to find which is best. Consider choice "A" – Certainly an employee may discuss his complaint with fellow employees, but no change or improvement can result, and the complaint remains unresolved. Choice "B" is a poor choice since the head of the organization probably does not know what assignment you have been given, and taking your problem to him is known as "going over the head" of the supervisor. The supervisor, or person who made the assignment, is the person who can clarify it or correct any injustice. Choice "C" is, therefore, correct. To say nothing, as in choice "D," is unwise. Supervisors have and interest in knowing the problems employees are facing, and the employee is seeking a solution to his problem.

2) True/False Questions

The "true/false" or "right/wrong" form of question is sometimes used. Here a complete statement is given. Your job is to decide whether the statement is right or wrong.

SAMPLE: A roaming cell-phone call to a nearby city costs less than a non-roaming call to a distant city.

This statement is wrong, or false, since roaming calls are more expensive.

This is not a complete list of all possible question forms, although most of the others are variations of these common types. You will always get complete directions for answering questions. Be sure you understand *how* to mark your answers – ask questions until you do.

V. RECORDING YOUR ANSWERS

Computer terminals are used more and more today for many different kinds of exams.

For an examination with very few applicants, you may be told to record your answers in the test booklet itself. Separate answer sheets are much more common. If this separate answer sheet is to be scored by machine – and this is often the case – it is highly important that you mark your answers correctly in order to get credit.

An electronic scoring machine is often used in civil service offices because of the speed with which papers can be scored. Machine-scored answer sheets must be marked with a pencil, which will be given to you. This pencil has a high graphite content which responds to the electronic scoring machine. As a matter of fact, stray dots may register as answers, so do not let your pencil rest on the answer sheet while you are pondering the correct answer. Also, if your pencil lead breaks or is otherwise defective, ask for another.

Since the answer sheet will be dropped in a slot in the scoring machine, be careful not to bend the corners or get the paper crumpled.

The answer sheet normally has five vertical columns of numbers, with 30 numbers to a column. These numbers correspond to the question numbers in your test booklet. After each number, going across the page are four or five pairs of dotted lines. These short dotted lines have small letters or numbers above them. The first two pairs may also have a "T" or "F" above the letters. This indicates that the first two pairs only are to be used if the questions are of the true-false type. If the questions are multiple choice, disregard the "T" and "F" and pay attention only to the small letters or numbers.

Answer your questions in the manner of the sample that follows:

32. The largest city in the United States is
    A. Washington, D.C.
    B. New York City
    C. Chicago
    D. Detroit
    E. San Francisco

1) Choose the answer you think is best. (New York City is the largest, so "B" is correct.)
2) Find the row of dotted lines numbered the same as the question you are answering. (Find row number 32)
3) Find the pair of dotted lines corresponding to the answer. (Find the pair of lines under the mark "B.")
4) Make a solid black mark between the dotted lines.

VI. BEFORE THE TEST

Common sense will help you find procedures to follow to get ready for an examination. Too many of us, however, overlook these sensible measures. Indeed, nervousness and fatigue have been found to be the most serious reasons why applicants fail to do their best on civil service tests. Here is a list of reminders:

- Begin your preparation early – Don't wait until the last minute to go scurrying around for books and materials or to find out what the position is all about.
- Prepare continuously – An hour a night for a week is better than an all-night cram session. This has been definitely established. What is more, a night a week for a month will return better dividends than crowding your study into a shorter period of time.
- Locate the place of the exam – You have been sent a notice telling you when and where to report for the examination. If the location is in a different town or otherwise unfamiliar to you, it would be well to inquire the best route and learn something about the building.
- Relax the night before the test – Allow your mind to rest. Do not study at all that night. Plan some mild recreation or diversion; then go to bed early and get a good night's sleep.
- Get up early enough to make a leisurely trip to the place for the test – This way unforeseen events, traffic snarls, unfamiliar buildings, etc. will not upset you.
- Dress comfortably – A written test is not a fashion show. You will be known by number and not by name, so wear something comfortable.

- Leave excess paraphernalia at home – Shopping bags and odd bundles will get in your way. You need bring only the items mentioned in the official notice you received; usually everything you need is provided. Do not bring reference books to the exam. They will only confuse those last minutes and be taken away from you when in the test room.
- Arrive somewhat ahead of time – If because of transportation schedules you must get there very early, bring a newspaper or magazine to take your mind off yourself while waiting.
- Locate the examination room – When you have found the proper room, you will be directed to the seat or part of the room where you will sit. Sometimes you are given a sheet of instructions to read while you are waiting. Do not fill out any forms until you are told to do so; just read them and be prepared.
- Relax and prepare to listen to the instructions
- If you have any physical problem that may keep you from doing your best, be sure to tell the test administrator. If you are sick or in poor health, you really cannot do your best on the exam. You can come back and take the test some other time.

VII. AT THE TEST

The day of the test is here and you have the test booklet in your hand. The temptation to get going is very strong. Caution! There is more to success than knowing the right answers. You must know how to identify your papers and understand variations in the type of short-answer question used in this particular examination. Follow these suggestions for maximum results from your efforts:

1) Cooperate with the monitor

The test administrator has a duty to create a situation in which you can be as much at ease as possible. He will give instructions, tell you when to begin, check to see that you are marking your answer sheet correctly, and so on. He is not there to guard you, although he will see that your competitors do not take unfair advantage. He wants to help you do your best.

2) Listen to all instructions

Don't jump the gun! Wait until you understand all directions. In most civil service tests you get more time than you need to answer the questions. So don't be in a hurry. Read each word of instructions until you clearly understand the meaning. Study the examples, listen to all announcements and follow directions. Ask questions if you do not understand what to do.

3) Identify your papers

Civil service exams are usually identified by number only. You will be assigned a number; you must not put your name on your test papers. Be sure to copy your number correctly. Since more than one exam may be given, copy your exact examination title.

4) Plan your time

Unless you are told that a test is a "speed" or "rate of work" test, speed itself is usually not important. Time enough to answer all the questions will be provided, but this does not mean that you have all day. An overall time limit has been set. Divide the total time (in minutes) by the number of questions to determine the approximate time you have for each question.

5) Do not linger over difficult questions

If you come across a difficult question, mark it with a paper clip (useful to have along) and come back to it when you have been through the booklet. One caution if you do this – be sure to skip a number on your answer sheet as well. Check often to be sure that you have not lost your place and that you are marking in the row numbered the same as the question you are answering.

6) Read the questions

Be sure you know what the question asks! Many capable people are unsuccessful because they failed to *read* the questions correctly.

7) Answer all questions

Unless you have been instructed that a penalty will be deducted for incorrect answers, it is better to guess than to omit a question.

8) Speed tests

It is often better NOT to guess on speed tests. It has been found that on timed tests people are tempted to spend the last few seconds before time is called in marking answers at random – without even reading them – in the hope of picking up a few extra points. To discourage this practice, the instructions may warn you that your score will be "corrected" for guessing. That is, a penalty will be applied. The incorrect answers will be deducted from the correct ones, or some other penalty formula will be used.

9) Review your answers

If you finish before time is called, go back to the questions you guessed or omitted to give them further thought. Review other answers if you have time.

10) Return your test materials

If you are ready to leave before others have finished or time is called, take ALL your materials to the monitor and leave quietly. Never take any test material with you. The monitor can discover whose papers are not complete, and taking a test booklet may be grounds for disqualification.

VIII. EXAMINATION TECHNIQUES

1) Read the general instructions carefully. These are usually printed on the first page of the exam booklet. As a rule, these instructions refer to the timing of the examination; the fact that you should not start work until the signal and must stop work at a signal, etc. If there are any *special* instructions, such as a choice of questions to be answered, make sure that you note this instruction carefully.

2) When you are ready to start work on the examination, that is as soon as the signal has been given, read the instructions to each question booklet, underline any key words or phrases, such as *least, best, outline, describe* and the like. In this way you will tend to answer as requested rather than discover on reviewing your paper that you *listed without describing*, that you selected the *worst* choice rather than the *best* choice, etc.

3) If the examination is of the objective or multiple-choice type – that is, each question will also give a series of possible answers: A, B, C or D, and you are called upon to select the best answer and write the letter next to that answer on your answer paper – it is advisable to start answering each question in turn. There may be anywhere from 50 to 100 such questions in the three or four hours allotted and you can see how much time would be taken if you read through all the questions before beginning to answer any. Furthermore, if you come across a question or group of questions which you know would be difficult to answer, it would undoubtedly affect your handling of all the other questions.

4) If the examination is of the essay type and contains but a few questions, it is a moot point as to whether you should read all the questions before starting to answer any one. Of course, if you are given a choice – say five out of seven and the like – then it is essential to read all the questions so you can eliminate the two that are most difficult. If, however, you are asked to answer all the questions, there may be danger in trying to answer the easiest one first because you may find that you will spend too much time on it. The best technique is to answer the first question, then proceed to the second, etc.

5) Time your answers. Before the exam begins, write down the time it started, then add the time allowed for the examination and write down the time it must be completed, then divide the time available somewhat as follows:
    - If 3-1/2 hours are allowed, that would be 210 minutes. If you have 80 objective-type questions, that would be an average of 2-1/2 minutes per question. Allow yourself no more than 2 minutes per question, or a total of 160 minutes, which will permit about 50 minutes to review.
    - If for the time allotment of 210 minutes there are 7 essay questions to answer, that would average about 30 minutes a question. Give yourself only 25 minutes per question so that you have about 35 minutes to review.

6) The most important instruction is to *read each question* and make sure you know what is wanted. The second most important instruction is to *time yourself properly* so that you answer every question. The third most important instruction is to *answer every question*. Guess if you have to but include something for each question. Remember that you will receive no credit for a blank and will probably receive some credit if you write something in answer to an essay question. If you guess a letter – say "B" for a multiple-choice question – you may have guessed right. If you leave a blank as an answer to a multiple-choice question, the examiners may respect your feelings but it will not add a point to your score. Some exams may penalize you for wrong answers, so in such cases *only*, you may not want to guess unless you have some basis for your answer.

7) Suggestions
    a. Objective-type questions
        1. Examine the question booklet for proper sequence of pages and questions
        2. Read all instructions carefully
        3. Skip any question which seems too difficult; return to it after all other questions have been answered
        4. Apportion your time properly; do not spend too much time on any single question or group of questions

5. Note and underline key words – *all, most, fewest, least, best, worst, same, opposite,* etc.
6. Pay particular attention to negatives
7. Note unusual option, e.g., unduly long, short, complex, different or similar in content to the body of the question
8. Observe the use of "hedging" words – *probably, may, most likely,* etc.
9. Make sure that your answer is put next to the same number as the question
10. Do not second-guess unless you have good reason to believe the second answer is definitely more correct
11. Cross out original answer if you decide another answer is more accurate; do not erase until you are ready to hand your paper in
12. Answer all questions; guess unless instructed otherwise
13. Leave time for review

b. Essay questions
1. Read each question carefully
2. Determine exactly what is wanted. Underline key words or phrases.
3. Decide on outline or paragraph answer
4. Include many different points and elements unless asked to develop any one or two points or elements
5. Show impartiality by giving pros and cons unless directed to select one side only
6. Make and write down any assumptions you find necessary to answer the questions
7. Watch your English, grammar, punctuation and choice of words
8. Time your answers; don't crowd material

8) Answering the essay question

Most essay questions can be answered by framing the specific response around several key words or ideas. Here are a few such key words or ideas:

M's: manpower, materials, methods, money, management
P's: purpose, program, policy, plan, procedure, practice, problems, pitfalls, personnel, public relations

a. Six basic steps in handling problems:
1. Preliminary plan and background development
2. Collect information, data and facts
3. Analyze and interpret information, data and facts
4. Analyze and develop solutions as well as make recommendations
5. Prepare report and sell recommendations
6. Install recommendations and follow up effectiveness

b. Pitfalls to avoid
1. *Taking things for granted* – A statement of the situation does not necessarily imply that each of the elements is necessarily true; for example, a complaint may be invalid and biased so that all that can be taken for granted is that a complaint has been registered

2. *Considering only one side of a situation* – Wherever possible, indicate several alternatives and then point out the reasons you selected the best one
3. *Failing to indicate follow up* – Whenever your answer indicates action on your part, make certain that you will take proper follow-up action to see how successful your recommendations, procedures or actions turn out to be
4. *Taking too long in answering any single question* – Remember to time your answers properly

IX. AFTER THE TEST

Scoring procedures differ in detail among civil service jurisdictions although the general principles are the same. Whether the papers are hand-scored or graded by machine we have described, they are nearly always graded by number. That is, the person who marks the paper knows only the number – never the name – of the applicant. Not until all the papers have been graded will they be matched with names. If other tests, such as training and experience or oral interview ratings have been given, scores will be combined. Different parts of the examination usually have different weights. For example, the written test might count 60 percent of the final grade, and a rating of training and experience 40 percent. In many jurisdictions, veterans will have a certain number of points added to their grades.

After the final grade has been determined, the names are placed in grade order and an eligible list is established. There are various methods for resolving ties between those who get the same final grade – probably the most common is to place first the name of the person whose application was received first. Job offers are made from the eligible list in the order the names appear on it. You will be notified of your grade and your rank as soon as all these computations have been made. This will be done as rapidly as possible.

People who are found to meet the requirements in the announcement are called "eligibles." Their names are put on a list of eligible candidates. An eligible's chances of getting a job depend on how high he stands on this list and how fast agencies are filling jobs from the list.

When a job is to be filled from a list of eligibles, the agency asks for the names of people on the list of eligibles for that job. When the civil service commission receives this request, it sends to the agency the names of the three people highest on this list. Or, if the job to be filled has specialized requirements, the office sends the agency the names of the top three persons who meet these requirements from the general list.

The appointing officer makes a choice from among the three people whose names were sent to him. If the selected person accepts the appointment, the names of the others are put back on the list to be considered for future openings.

That is the rule in hiring from all kinds of eligible lists, whether they are for typist, carpenter, chemist, or something else. For every vacancy, the appointing officer has his choice of any one of the top three eligibles on the list. This explains why the person whose name is on top of the list sometimes does not get an appointment when some of the persons lower on the list do. If the appointing officer chooses the second or third eligible, the No. 1 eligible does not get a job at once, but stays on the list until he is appointed or the list is terminated.

X. HOW TO PASS THE INTERVIEW TEST

The examination for which you applied requires an oral interview test. You have already taken the written test and you are now being called for the interview test – the final part of the formal examination.

You may think that it is not possible to prepare for an interview test and that there are no procedures to follow during an interview. Our purpose is to point out some things you can do in advance that will help you and some good rules to follow and pitfalls to avoid while you are being interviewed.

What is an interview supposed to test?

The written examination is designed to test the technical knowledge and competence of the candidate; the oral is designed to evaluate intangible qualities, not readily measured otherwise, and to establish a list showing the relative fitness of each candidate – as measured against his competitors – for the position sought. Scoring is not on the basis of "right" and "wrong," but on a sliding scale of values ranging from "not passable" to "outstanding." As a matter of fact, it is possible to achieve a relatively low score without a single "incorrect" answer because of evident weakness in the qualities being measured.

Occasionally, an examination may consist entirely of an oral test – either an individual or a group oral. In such cases, information is sought concerning the technical knowledges and abilities of the candidate, since there has been no written examination for this purpose. More commonly, however, an oral test is used to supplement a written examination.

Who conducts interviews?

The composition of oral boards varies among different jurisdictions. In nearly all, a representative of the personnel department serves as chairman. One of the members of the board may be a representative of the department in which the candidate would work. In some cases, "outside experts" are used, and, frequently, a businessman or some other representative of the general public is asked to serve. Labor and management or other special groups may be represented. The aim is to secure the services of experts in the appropriate field.

However the board is composed, it is a good idea (and not at all improper or unethical) to ascertain in advance of the interview who the members are and what groups they represent. When you are introduced to them, you will have some idea of their backgrounds and interests, and at least you will not stutter and stammer over their names.

What should be done before the interview?

While knowledge about the board members is useful and takes some of the surprise element out of the interview, there is other preparation which is more substantive. It *is* possible to prepare for an oral interview – in several ways:

1) Keep a copy of your application and review it carefully before the interview

This may be the only document before the oral board, and the starting point of the interview. Know what education and experience you have listed there, and the sequence and dates of all of it. Sometimes the board will ask you to review the highlights of your experience for them; you should not have to hem and haw doing it.

2) Study the class specification and the examination announcement

Usually, the oral board has one or both of these to guide them. The qualities, characteristics or knowledges required by the position sought are stated in these documents. They offer valuable clues as to the nature of the oral interview. For example, if the job involves supervisory responsibilities, the announcement will usually indicate that knowledge of modern supervisory methods and the qualifications of the candidate as a supervisor will be tested. If so, you can expect such questions, frequently in the form of a hypothetical situation which you are expected to solve. NEVER go into an oral without knowledge of the duties and responsibilities of the job you seek.

3) Think through each qualification required

Try to visualize the kind of questions you would ask if you were a board member. How well could you answer them? Try especially to appraise your own knowledge and background in each area, *measured against the job sought*, and identify any areas in which you are weak. Be critical and realistic – do not flatter yourself.

4) Do some general reading in areas in which you feel you may be weak

For example, if the job involves supervision and your past experience has NOT, some general reading in supervisory methods and practices, particularly in the field of human relations, might be useful. Do NOT study agency procedures or detailed manuals. The oral board will be testing your understanding and capacity, not your memory.

5) Get a good night's sleep and watch your general health and mental attitude

You will want a clear head at the interview. Take care of a cold or any other minor ailment, and of course, no hangovers.

What should be done on the day of the interview?

Now comes the day of the interview itself. Give yourself plenty of time to get there. Plan to arrive somewhat ahead of the scheduled time, particularly if your appointment is in the fore part of the day. If a previous candidate fails to appear, the board might be ready for you a bit early. By early afternoon an oral board is almost invariably behind schedule if there are many candidates, and you may have to wait. Take along a book or magazine to read, or your application to review, but leave any extraneous material in the waiting room when you go in for your interview. In any event, relax and compose yourself.

The matter of dress is important. The board is forming impressions about you – from your experience, your manners, your attitude, and your appearance. Give your personal appearance careful attention. Dress your best, but not your flashiest. Choose conservative, appropriate clothing, and be sure it is immaculate. This is a business interview, and your appearance should indicate that you regard it as such. Besides, being well groomed and properly dressed will help boost your confidence.

Sooner or later, someone will call your name and escort you into the interview room. *This is it.* From here on you are on your own. It is too late for any more preparation. But remember, you asked for this opportunity to prove your fitness, and you are here because your request was granted.

What happens when you go in?

The usual sequence of events will be as follows: The clerk (who is often the board stenographer) will introduce you to the chairman of the oral board, who will introduce you to the other members of the board. Acknowledge the introductions before you sit down. Do not be surprised if you find a microphone facing you or a stenotypist sitting by. Oral interviews are usually recorded in the event of an appeal or other review.

Usually the chairman of the board will open the interview by reviewing the highlights of your education and work experience from your application – primarily for the benefit of the other members of the board, as well as to get the material into the record. Do not interrupt or comment unless there is an error or significant misinterpretation; if that is the case, do not hesitate. But do not quibble about insignificant matters. Also, he will usually ask you some question about your education, experience or your present job – partly to get you to start talking and to establish the interviewing "rapport." He may start the actual questioning, or turn it over to one of the other members. Frequently, each member undertakes the questioning on a particular area, one in which he is perhaps most competent, so you can expect each member to participate in the examination. Because time is limited, you may also expect some rather abrupt switches in the direction the questioning takes, so do not be upset by it. Normally, a board member will not pursue a single line of questioning unless he discovers a particular strength or weakness.

After each member has participated, the chairman will usually ask whether any member has any further questions, then will ask you if you have anything you wish to add. Unless you are expecting this question, it may floor you. Worse, it may start you off on an extended, extemporaneous speech. The board is not usually seeking more information. The question is principally to offer you a last opportunity to present further qualifications or to indicate that you have nothing to add. So, if you feel that a significant qualification or characteristic has been overlooked, it is proper to point it out in a sentence or so. Do not compliment the board on the thoroughness of their examination – they have been sketchy, and you know it. If you wish, merely say, "No thank you, I have nothing further to add." This is a point where you can "talk yourself out" of a good impression or fail to present an important bit of information. Remember, *you close the interview yourself.*

The chairman will then say, "That is all, Mr. _____, thank you." Do not be startled; the interview is over, and quicker than you think. Thank him, gather your belongings and take your leave. Save your sigh of relief for the other side of the door.

How to put your best foot forward

Throughout this entire process, you may feel that the board individually and collectively is trying to pierce your defenses, seek out your hidden weaknesses and embarrass and confuse you. Actually, this is not true. They are obliged to make an appraisal of your qualifications for the job you are seeking, and they want to see you in your best light. Remember, they must interview all candidates and a non-cooperative candidate may become a failure in spite of their best efforts to bring out his qualifications. Here are 15 suggestions that will help you:

1) Be natural – Keep your attitude confident, not cocky

If you are not confident that you can do the job, do not expect the board to be. Do not apologize for your weaknesses, try to bring out your strong points. The board is interested in a positive, not negative, presentation. Cockiness will antagonize any board member and make him wonder if you are covering up a weakness by a false show of strength.

2) Get comfortable, but don't lounge or sprawl

Sit erectly but not stiffly. A careless posture may lead the board to conclude that you are careless in other things, or at least that you are not impressed by the importance of the occasion. Either conclusion is natural, even if incorrect. Do not fuss with your clothing, a pencil or an ashtray. Your hands may occasionally be useful to emphasize a point; do not let them become a point of distraction.

3) Do not wisecrack or make small talk

This is a serious situation, and your attitude should show that you consider it as such. Further, the time of the board is limited – they do not want to waste it, and neither should you.

4) Do not exaggerate your experience or abilities

In the first place, from information in the application or other interviews and sources, the board may know more about you than you think. Secondly, you probably will not get away with it. An experienced board is rather adept at spotting such a situation, so do not take the chance.

5) If you know a board member, do not make a point of it, yet do not hide it

Certainly you are not fooling him, and probably not the other members of the board. Do not try to take advantage of your acquaintanceship – it will probably do you little good.

6) Do not dominate the interview

Let the board do that. They will give you the clues – do not assume that you have to do all the talking. Realize that the board has a number of questions to ask you, and do not try to take up all the interview time by showing off your extensive knowledge of the answer to the first one.

7) Be attentive

You only have 20 minutes or so, and you should keep your attention at its sharpest throughout. When a member is addressing a problem or question to you, give him your undivided attention. Address your reply principally to him, but do not exclude the other board members.

8) Do not interrupt

A board member may be stating a problem for you to analyze. He will ask you a question when the time comes. Let him state the problem, and wait for the question.

9) Make sure you understand the question

Do not try to answer until you are sure what the question is. If it is not clear, restate it in your own words or ask the board member to clarify it for you. However, do not haggle about minor elements.

10) Reply promptly but not hastily

A common entry on oral board rating sheets is "candidate responded readily," or "candidate hesitated in replies." Respond as promptly and quickly as you can, but do not jump to a hasty, ill-considered answer.

11) Do not be peremptory in your answers

A brief answer is proper – but do not fire your answer back. That is a losing game from your point of view. The board member can probably ask questions much faster than you can answer them.

12) Do not try to create the answer you think the board member wants

He is interested in what kind of mind you have and how it works – not in playing games. Furthermore, he can usually spot this practice and will actually grade you down on it.

13) Do not switch sides in your reply merely to agree with a board member

Frequently, a member will take a contrary position merely to draw you out and to see if you are willing and able to defend your point of view. Do not start a debate, yet do not surrender a good position. If a position is worth taking, it is worth defending.

14) Do not be afraid to admit an error in judgment if you are shown to be wrong

The board knows that you are forced to reply without any opportunity for careful consideration. Your answer may be demonstrably wrong. If so, admit it and get on with the interview.

15) Do not dwell at length on your present job

The opening question may relate to your present assignment. Answer the question but do not go into an extended discussion. You are being examined for a *new* job, not your present one. As a matter of fact, try to phrase ALL your answers in terms of the job for which you are being examined.

Basis of Rating

Probably you will forget most of these "do's" and "don'ts" when you walk into the oral interview room. Even remembering them all will not ensure you a passing grade. Perhaps you did not have the qualifications in the first place. But remembering them will help you to put your best foot forward, without treading on the toes of the board members.

Rumor and popular opinion to the contrary notwithstanding, an oral board wants you to make the best appearance possible. They know you are under pressure – but they also want to see how you respond to it as a guide to what your reaction would be under the pressures of the job you seek. They will be influenced by the degree of poise you display, the personal traits you show and the manner in which you respond.

ABOUT THIS BOOK

This book contains tests divided into Examination Sections. Go through each test, answering every question in the margin. We have also attached a sample answer sheet at the back of the book that can be removed and used. At the end of each test look at the answer key and check your answers. On the ones you got wrong, look at the right answer choice and learn. Do not fill in the answers first. Do not memorize the questions and answers, but understand the answer and principles involved. On your test, the questions will likely be different from the samples. Questions are changed and new ones added. If you understand these past questions you should have success with any changes that arise. Tests may consist of several types of questions. We have additional books on each subject should more study be advisable or necessary for you. Finally, the more you study, the better prepared you will be. This book is intended to be the last thing you study before you walk into the examination room. Prior study of relevant texts is also recommended. NLC publishes some of these in our Fundamental Series. Knowledge and good sense are important factors in passing your exam. Good luck also helps. So now study this Passbook, absorb the material contained within and take that knowledge into the examination. Then do your best to pass that exam.

EXAMINATION SECTION

EXAMINATION SECTION
TEST 1

DIRECTIONS: Each question or incomplete statement is followed by several suggested answers or completions. Select the one that BEST answers the question or completes the statement. *PRINT THE LETTER OF THE CORRECT ANSWER IN THE SPACE AT THE RIGHT.*

1. The process of determining the quantity of goods and materials that are in stock is commonly called

    A. receiving
    B. disbursement
    C. reconciliation
    D. inventory

    1.____

2. Proper and effective storage procedure involves the storing of

    A. items together on the basis of class grouping
    B. all items in chronological order based on date received
    C. items in alphabetical order based on date of delivery
    D. items randomly wherever space is available

    2.____

3. Which of the following is the FIRST step involved in correctly taking an inventory?

    A. Reconciliation of inventory records with the number of items on hand
    B. Analysis of possible discrepancies between items on hand and the stock record balance
    C. Identification and recording of the locations of all items in stock
    D. Issuance of an inventory directive to all vendors

    3.____

4. Supply items other than food which are subject to deterioration should be checked

    A. at delivery time only
    B. occasionally
    C. only when issued
    D. periodically

    4.____

5. For which of the following supplies is it MOST necessary to provide ample ventilation?

    A. Small rubber parts
    B. Metal products
    C. Flammable liquids
    D. Wooden items

    5.____

6. Storing small lots of supplies in an area designated for the storage of large lots of supplies will generally result in

    A. *loss* of supplies
    B. *loss* of storage space
    C. *increase* in inventory
    D. *increase* in storage space

    6.____

7. Compliance with fire preventive measures is a major requirement for the maintenance of a safe warehouse. Which of the following statements is LEAST important in describing a measure useful in maintaining a fire preventive facility?

    A. Smoking is only permitted in designated areas.
    B. Oil-soaked rags should be disposed of promptly and not stored.
    C. When not in use, electrical machinery should be grounded.
    D. Gasoline-powered materials handling equipment should not be refueled with the motor running.

    7.____

8. It is POOR storage practice to store small valuable items loosely in open containers in bulk storage areas because doing so results in the

   A. misplacement of such items
   B. pilferage of these items
   C. deterioration of such supplies
   D. hindrance in inspection of these supplies

9. Assume that you have been placed in charge of the receiving operations at your garage. Generally, you receive all the supplies you order during the first week of each month. Of the following, the MOST effective and economic way to facilitate receiving operations would be to

   A. secure overtime authorization for laborers during that week
   B. have all truck deliveries made in one day
   C. stagger truck deliveries throughout each morning of the week
   D. assign all personnel to receiving duty for that week

10. Effective security measures must be instituted to provide for the safekeeping of city supplies.
    However, the scope and complexity of security measures used at a warehouse facility should correspond MOST NEARLY to the

    A. value of supplies stored in the warehouse
    B. borough in which the warehouse is located
    C. level of warehouse activity
    D. age of the warehouse facility

11. To facilitate handling and issuance of supply items that have a high turnover rate, they should generally be stored

    A. away from accessible aisles
    B. on upper shelves
    C. in a locked compartment area
    D. close to the service counter area

12. The MOST important factor to be considered in effectively storing heavy, bulky, and difficult-to-handle items is to store these items

    A. as close to shipping areas as possible
    B. in storage areas with a low floor-load capacity
    C. only in outside storage sheds
    D. away from aisles

Questions 13-16.

DIRECTIONS: Questions 13 through 16 are to be answered using ONLY the information in the following passage.

Fire exit drills should be established and held periodically to effectively train personnel to leave their working area promptly upon proper signal and to evacuate the building speedily but without confusion. All fire exit drills should be carefully planned and carried out in a serious manner under rigid discipline so as to provide positive protection in the event of a real emergency. As a general rule, the local fire department should be furnished advance information regarding the exact date and time the exit drill is scheduled. When it is impossible to hold regular drills, written instructions should be distributed to all employees.

Depending upon individual circumstances, fires in warehouses vary from those of fast development that are almost instantly beyond any possibility of employee control to others of relatively slow development where a small readily attackable flame may be present for periods of time up to 15 minutes or more during which simple attack with fire extinguishers or small building hoses may prevent the fire development. In any case, it is characteristic of many warehouse fires that at a certain point in development they flash up to the top of the stack, increase heat quickly, and spread rapidly. There is a degree of inherent danger in attacking warehouse type fires and all employees should be thoroughly trained in the use of the types of extinguishers or small hoses in the buildings and well instructed in the necessity of always staying between the fire and a direct pass to an exit.

13. Employees should be instructed that, when fighting a fire, they MUST

    A. try to control the blaze
    B. extinguish any fire in 15 minutes
    C. remain between the fire and a direct passage to the exit
    D. keep the fire between themselves and the fire exit

14. Whenever conditions are such that regular fire drills cannot be held, then which one of the following actions should be taken?

    A. The local fire department should be notified.
    B. Rigid discipline should be maintained during work hours.
    C. Personnel should be instructed to leave their working area by whatever means are available.
    D. Employees should receive fire drill procedures in writing.

15. The passage indicates that the purpose of fire exit drills is to train employees to

    A. control a fire before it becomes uncontrollable
    B. act as firefighters
    C. leave the working area promptly
    D. be serious

16. According to the passage, fire exit drills will prove to be of *utmost* effectiveness if

    A. employee participation is made voluntary
    B. they take place periodically
    C. the fire department actively participates
    D. they are held without advance planning

Questions 17-20.

DIRECTIONS: Questions 17 through 20 are to be answered using ONLY the information in the following paragraph.

A report is frequently ineffective because the person writing it is not fully acquainted with all the necessary details before he actually starts to construct the report. All details pertaining to the subject should be known before the report is started. If the essential facts are not known, they should be investigated. It is wise to have essential facts written down rather than to depend too much on memory, especially if the facts pertain to such matters as amounts, dates, names of persons, or other specific data. When the necessary information has been gathered, the general plan and content of the report should be thought out before the writing is actually begun. A person with little or no experience in writing reports may find that it is wise to make a brief outline. Persons with more experience should not need a written outline, but they should make mental notes of the steps they are to follow. If writing reports without dictation is a regular part of an office worker's duties, he should set aside a certain time during the day when he is least likely to be interrupted. That may be difficult, but in most offices there are certain times in the day when the callers, telephone calls, and other interruptions are not numerous. During those times, it is best to write reports that need undivided concentration. Reports that are written amid a series of interruptions may be poorly done.

17. Before starting to write an effective report, it is necessary to

    A. memorize all specific information
    B. disregard ambiguous data
    C. know all pertinent information
    D. develop a general plan

18. Reports dealing with complex and difficult material should be

    A. prepared and written by the supervisor of the unit
    B. written when there is the least chance of interruption
    C. prepared and written as part of regular office routine
    D. outlined and then dictated

19. According to the passage, employees with no prior familiarity in writing reports may find it helpful to

    A. prepare a brief outline
    B. mentally prepare a synopsis of the report's content
    C. have a fellow employee help in writing the report
    D. consult previous reports

20. In writing a report, needed information which is unclear should be

    A. disregarded   B. investigated
    C. memorized   D. gathered

KEY (CORRECT ANSWERS)

1. D
2. A
3. C
4. D
5. C

6. B
7. C
8. B
9. C
10. A

11. D
12. A
13. C
14. D
15. C

16. B
17. C
18. B
19. A
20. B

TEST 2

DIRECTIONS: Each question or incomplete statement is followed by several suggested answers or completions. Select the one that BEST answers the question or completes the statement. *PRINT THE LETTER OF THE CORRECT ANSWER IN THE SPACE AT THE RIGHT.*

Questions 1-4.

DIRECTIONS: Questions 1 through 4 are to be answered using ONLY the information in the following passage.

The operation and maintenance of the stock-location system is a warehousing function and responsibility. The stock locator system shall consist of a file of stock-location record cards, either manually or mechanically prepared, depending upon the equipment available. The file shall contain an individual card for each stock item stored in the depot, with the records maintained in stock number sequence.

The locator file is used for all receiving, warehousing, inventory, and shipping activities in the depot. The locator file must contain complete and accurate data to provide ready support to the various depot functions and activities, i.e., processing shipping documents, updating records on mechanized equipment, where applicable, supplying accurate locator information for stock selection and proper storage of receipts, consolidating storage locations of identical items not subject to shelf-life control, and preventing the consolidation of stock of limited shelf-life items. The file is also essential in accomplishing location surveys and the inventory program.

Storage of bulk stock items by "spot-location" method is generally recognized as the best means of obtaining maximum warehouse space utilization. Despite the fact that the spot-location method of storage enables full utilization of storage capacity, this method may prove inefficient unless it is supplemented by adequate stock-location control, including proper lay-out and accurate maintenance of stock locator cards.

1. The manner in which the stock-location record cards should be filed is

   A. alphabetically
   B. chronologically
   C. numerically
   D. randomly

2. Items of limited shelf-life should

   A. not be stored
   B. not be stored together
   C. be stored in stock sequence
   D. be stored together

3. Which one of the following is NOT mentioned in the passage as a use of the stock-location system?
   Aids in

   A. accomplishing location surveys
   B. providing information for stock selection
   C. storing items received for the first time
   D. processing shipping documents

4. If the spot-location method of storing is used, then the use of the stock-location system is 4._____

   A. *desirable,* because the stock-location system is recognized as the best means of obtaining maximum warehouse space utilization
   B. *undesirable,* because additional records must be kept
   C. *desirable,* because stock-location controls are necessary with the spot-location storage method
   D. *undesirable,* because a stock-locator system will take up valuable storage space

Questions 5-8.

DIRECTIONS: Questions 5 through 8 are to be answered using ONLY the information in the following paragraph.

Known damage is defined as damage that is apparent and acknowledged by the carrier at the time of delivery to the purchaser. A meticulous inspection of the damaged goods should be completed by the purchaser and a notation specifying the extent of the damage should be applied to the carrier's original freight bill. As is the case in known loss, it is necessary for the carrier's agent to acknowledge by signature the damage notation in order for it to have any legal status. The purchaser should not refuse damaged freight since it is his legal duty to accept the property and to employ every available and reasonable means to protect the shipment and minimize the loss. Acceptance of a damaged shipment does not endanger any legitimate claim the purchaser may have against the carrier for damage. If the purchaser fails to observe the legal duty to accept damaged freight, the carrier may consider it abandoned. After properly notifying the vendor and purchaser of his intentions, the carrier may dispose of the material at public sale.

5. Before disposing of an abandoned shipment, the carrier must 5._____

   A. notify the vendor and the carrier's agent
   B. advise the vendor and purchaser of his plans
   C. notify the purchaser and the carrier's agent
   D. obtain the signature of the carrier's agent on the freight bill

6. In the case of damaged freight, the original freight bill will only have legal value if it is signed by the 6._____

   A. carrier's agent   B. purchaser
   C. vendor   D. purchaser and vendor

7. A purchaser does not protect a shipment of cargo that is damaged and is further deteriorating. 7._____
   According to the above paragraph, the action of the purchaser is

   A. *acceptable,* because he is not obligated to protect damaged cargo
   B. *unacceptable,* because damaged cargo must be protected no matter what is involved
   C. *acceptable,* because he took possession of the cargo
   D. *unacceptable,* because he is obligated by law to protect the cargo

8. The TWO requirements that must be satisfied before cargo can be labeled *known damage* are signs of evident damage and

   A. confirmation by the carrier or carrier's agent that this is so
   B. delayed shipment of goods
   C. signature of acceptance by the purchaser
   D. acknowledgment by the vendor that this is so

Questions 9-13.

DIRECTIONS: Questions 9 through 13 are to be answered on the basis of the following graph.

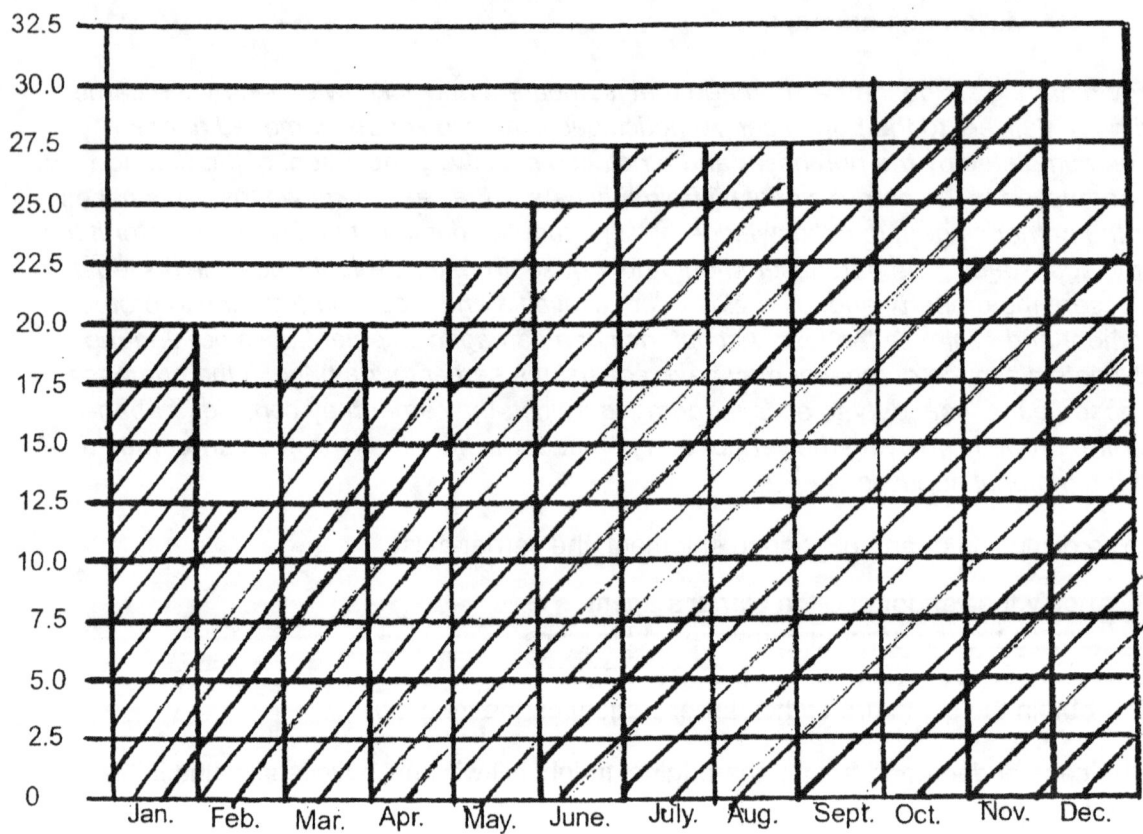

9. According to the information presented in the graph, the weight of the average monthly collection of garbage is MOST NEARLY _____ tons.

   A. 22.5   B. 23.5   C. 24.5   D. 25.5

10. If a truck can carry 6,000 lbs., then the number of truck-loads collected during the year was MOST NEARLY

    A. 55   B. 75   C. 95   D. 115

11. The amount of garbage collected during the second half of the year represents APPROXIMATELY what percentage of the total garbage collected during the year?

    A. 50%   B. 60%   C. 70%   D. 80%

12. During the months of September, October, and November, approximately 12% of the collections consisted of fallen leaves.
    What was the weight of the remaining garbage NOT containing fallen leaves for that period?
    _____ tons.
    A. 10   B. 20   C. 65   D. 75

13. Assume that the collections for the year as shown in the above graph exceeded the previous year's collection by 17%. The collection made in the previous year was MOST NEARLY _____ tons.
    A. 50   B. 225   C. 240   D. 275

Questions 14-17.

DIRECTIONS: Questions 14 through 17 are to be answered on the basis of the following graph

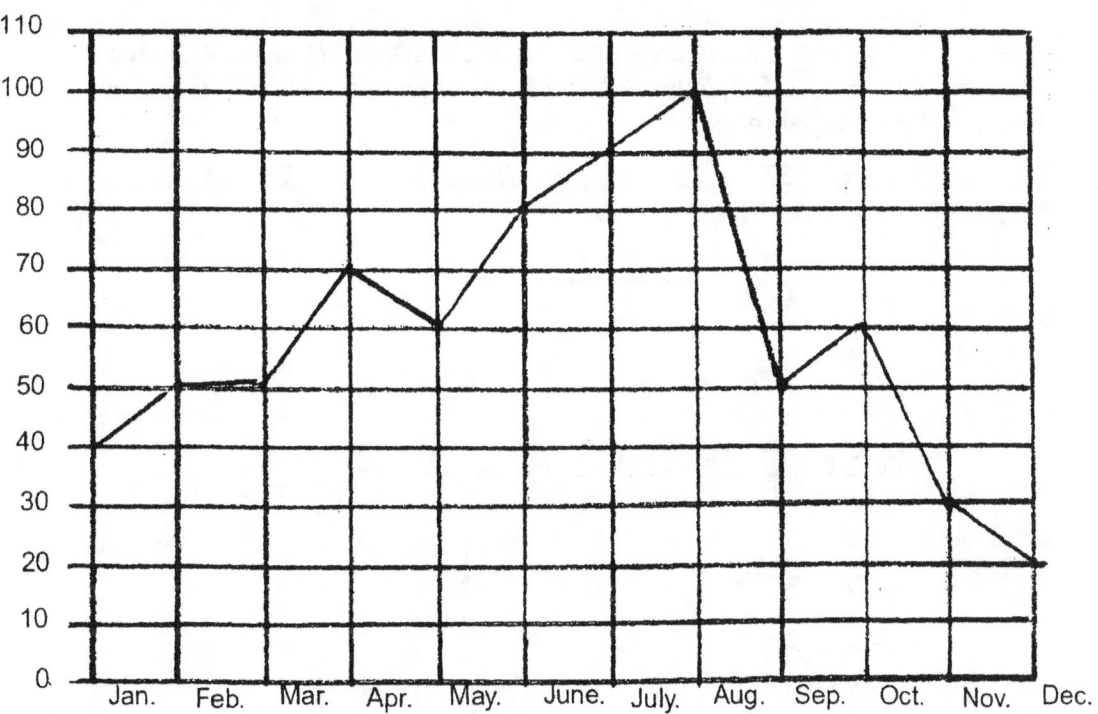

14. The average monthly inventory level during the course of the year was MOST NEARLY _____ dozen.
    A. 45   B. 60   C. 75   D. 90

15. If one dozen items fit in a carton measuring 2 feet by 2 feet by 3 feet, what MINIMUM volume would be required to store the maximum August inventory?
    _____ cubic feet.
    A. 12   B. 100   C. 700   D. 1,200

16. Assume that deliveries are made to the storehouse on the first working day of each month. If 30% of the June inventory was consumed during the month, how many items had to be delivered to reach the July inventory level?
  _____ items.

    A. 288   B. 408   C. 696   D. 1,080

17. Which three-month period contained the LOWEST average inventory level?

    A. Jan., Feb., March
    B. April, May, June
    C. July, Aug., Sept.
    D. Oct., Nov., Dec.

18. Assume that it takes approximately 1 1/2 minutes to unload a dozen identical items from a delivery truck.
    At this speed, the amount of time it should take to unload a shipment of 876 items is MOST NEARLY _____ minutes.

    A. 90   B. 100   C. 110   D. 120

19. Assume that a shop clerk has received a bill of $108 for a delivery of clamps which cost $4.32 per dozen.
    How many clamps should there be in this delivery?

    A. 25   B. 36   C. 300   D. 360

20. Employee A has not used any leave time and has accumulated a total of 45 leave days. How many months did it take Employee A to have accumulated 45 leave days if the accrual rate is 1 2/3 days per month?

    A. 25   B. 27   C. 29   D. 31

KEY (CORRECT ANSWERS)

1.	C	11.	B
2.	B	12.	D
3.	C	13.	C
4.	C	14.	B
5.	B	15.	D
6.	A	16.	B
7.	D	17.	D
8.	A	18.	C
9.	B	19.	C
10.	C	20.	B

EXAMINATION SECTION
TEST 1

DIRECTIONS: Each question or incomplete statement is followed by several suggested answers or completions. Select the one that BEST answers the question or completes the statement. *PRINT THE LETTER OF THE CORRECT ANSWER IN THE SPACE AT THE RIGHT.*

Questions 1-4.

DIRECTIONS: Questions 1 through 4 are to be answered using only the information in the following passage.

Planning for storage layout in terms of the supplies to be stored involves the intelligent and realistic application of a stockman's basic resources - space. The main objective of storage planning is the maximum use of available space. The planning and layout of space are dependent upon the types of supplies expected to be stored, and certain characteristics must be considered. Some supplies must be protected from dampness, extreme changes of temperature, and other such conditions. Iron and steel products rust quickly at high temperatures with high humidity. High temperatures also cause some plastics to melt and change shape, while extreme dampness can cause paper to mildew and wood to warp. Hazardous articles, including flammable items like paint and rubber cement, should be stored separated from each other and from other types of supplies.

Extremes in characteristics such as size, shape, and weight need to be considered in laying out space. Large, awkward containers and unusually heavy items generally should be stored near doors with aisles leading directly to them and/or shipping and receiving facilities. Light and fragile items cannot be stacked to a height which would cause crushing or other damage to containers and contents. Fast-moving articles should be stored in locations from which they can be handled quickly and efficiently.

1. It is MOST important to store articles like paints and rubber cement in areas where
    A. they can be protected from theft
    B. shipping and receiving doors are easily accessible
    C. they can be isolated from other supplies
    D. boxes containing them can be stacked as high as possible

2. Storage locations from which items can be selected and issued quickly are recommended for supplies classified as
    A. fragile   B. fast-moving
    C. under-sized   D. flammable

3. In order to prevent supplies made of iron from rusting, they should be stored in areas with _____ humidity and _____ temperature.
    A. low; high   B. low; low
    C. high; high   D. high; low

4. Which of the following characteristics is NOT considered in the above passage on storage planning and layout?
   The _____ of the item to be stored.
    A. size   B. quantity   C. weight   D. shape

1._____

2._____

3._____

4._____

11

Questions 5-12.

DIRECTIONS: Each of Questions 5 through 12 consists of a word in capitals followed by four suggested meanings of the word. For each question, choose the meaning which you think is BEST and print the letter of the correct answer in the space at the right.

5. CATALOG 5.____
   A. to list   B. to rate   C. to print   D. to price

6. DURABLE 6.____
   A. smooth   B. sticky   C. lasting   D. feeling

7. MUTUAL 7.____
   A. silent   B. shared   C. changing   D. broken

8. REJECT 8.____
   A. rewrite   B. refuse   C. release   D. regret

9. OBSTRUCT 9.____
   A. teach   B. darken   C. block   D. resist

10. CORRODE 10.____
   A. melt   B. rust   C. burn   D. warp

11. EXCESS 11.____
   A. surplus   B. storage   C. spacing   D. survey

12. FLEXIBLE 12.____
   A. neatly folded   B. easily broken
   C. easily bent   D. neatly piled

Questions 13-16.

DIRECTIONS: Questions 13 through 16 are to be answered using ONLY the information in the following passage.

The "active stock" portion of the inventory is that portion which is kept for the purpose of satisfying the shop's expected requirements of that material. It is directly related to the "order quantity." The "order quantity" is found by determining the expected annual requirements of the shop and dividing this by the number of orders for this merchandise which will be placed during the year. The most economical number of orders is usually found by considering the cost of ordering and storing inventory.

The "safety stock" portion of the inventory is that portion which is created to take care of above-average or unexpected demands on the inventory. This portion is directly related to the point at which the order is placed. The amount of safety stock is not determined by comparing order costs and carrying costs, but on the need for protection against stock shortages for each stock item under consideration. Some stock items will need more safety stock than others, depending upon how much difference there has been in the past between the expected usage of material and the actual amount needed and used for any given time period, plus the reliability of the suppliers' delivery and of the order lead-time. If the expected usage of an item has always been 100% accurately predicted, then theoretically there would be no need for "safety stock."

13. According to the above passage, the *active stock* inventory is that portion of the inventory which is

    A. used most frequently by management
    B. ordered on a regular basis, such as every month
    C. expected to meet the organization's anticipated inventory needs
    D. needed to protect against shortages in very active inventory items

14. According to the above passage, what factors must be considered to determine the order quantity for any active stock item?

    A. Anticipated requirements, ordering cost, and cost of storing inventory
    B. Order lead-time and delivery service
    C. Variety of stock items ordered in the previous year
    D. The largest quantity ever ordered

15. Maintaining a safety stock portion of the inventory is

    A. *good,* because it provides for unexpected demands on the inventory
    B. *good,* because it makes the inventory more valuable than it actually is
    C. *poor,* because it provides unnecessary work for stockmen since the Inventory is rarely used
    D. *poor,* because it makes storage areas overcrowded and unsafe

16. The above passage indicates that 100 percent accuracy in forecasting future activity will eliminate the need for

    A. reliable deliveries
    B. active stock
    C. safety stock
    D. deviation in total order quantity

17. At the start of a certain month, you have 185 jars of glue in stock. During that month, you fill the following orders: 3 orders for 12 jars each, 2 orders for 10 jars each, 2 orders for 8 jars each, one order for 9 jars, one order for 20 jars, and one order for 24 jars.
    If you received no shipments of glue during that month, the number of jars of glue you will have on hand at the end of the month is

    A. 60   B. 77   C. 102   D. 125

18. Assume that you are ordering merchandise from a vendor who gives a discount of 10%, plus an additional 2% for payment within 30 days.
    If, on October 21st, you order merchandise which has a catalogue value of $714, and the bill is paid by November 10th, the net amount of the payment should be MOST NEARLY

    A. $628.32   B. $629.95   C. $630.74   D. $632.60

19. Suppose that there are 293 people in your shop and 11% of them are women. 19.____
    The number of men in your shop is

    A. 261 B. 263 C. 269 D. 271

20. In March, Department Z made an overpayment of $34.26 to the Superior Fuel Oil Company. This amount was credited to the Department's account. In April, the fuel bill amounted to $378.12. 20.____
    Considering the credit on the Department's account, the payment that should be remitted for the April fuel bill is

    A. $343.86 B. $343.96 C. $344.86 D. $344.96

21. A certain agency ordered and used 1,020 one-pound balls of twine last year at a total cost of $357. 21.____
    If the price per ball of twine remained constant throughout the year, the cost of each one-pound ball was

    A. 25¢ B. 30¢ C. 35¢ D. 40¢

22. You place an order at the Abbey Office Supply Company for three of each of the following items: metal desk at $129 each; chair at $65 each; desk lamp at $24 each. 22.____
    If this supply company gives a 15% discount on all orders totaling $500 or more, the net price of this order is

    A. $567.90 B. $555.90 C. $484.20 D. $479.20

23. Suppose that there are 27 people in your department and your boss tells you that he is putting on an extra laborer and two mechanics. 23.____
    The percent of the increase in personnel for your department would be MOST NEARLY

    A. 8% B. 9% C. 10% D. 11%

Questions 24-29.

DIRECTIONS:

CODE TABLE

Code Letter	b	d	f	a	g	s	z	w	h	u
Code Number	1	2	3	4	5	6	7	8	9	0

In the Code Table above, each code letter has a corresponding code number directly beneath it.

Each of Questions 24 through 29 contains three sets of code letters and code numbers. In each set, the code numbers should correspond with the code letters as given in the table, but there is a coding error in some of the sets. Examine the sets in each question carefully.

Mark your answer:
A if there is a coding error in only ONE of the sets in the question;
B if there is a coding error in any TWO of the sets in the question;
C if there is a coding error in all THREE sets in the question;
D if there is a coding error in NONE of the sets in the question.

SAMPLE QUESTION:

fgzduwaf - 35720843
uabsdgfw - 04262538
hhfaudgs - 99340257

In the sample question above, the first set is right because each code number matches the code letter as in the Code Table. In the second set, the corresponding number for the code letter b is wrong because it should be 1 instead of 2. In the third set, the corresponding number for the last code letter s is wrong because it should be 6 instead of 7. Since there is an error in two of the sets, the answer to the above sample question is B.

24. fsbughwz - 36104987
    zwubgasz - 78025467
    ghgufddb - 59583221

25. hafgdaas - 94351446
    ddsfabsd - 22734162
    wgdbssgf - 85216553

26. abfbssbd - 41316712
    ghzfaubs - 59734017
    sdbzfwza - 62173874

27. whfbdzag - 89412745
    daaszuub - 24467001
    uzhfwssd - 07936623

28. zbadgbuh - 71425109
    dzadbbsz - 27421167
    gazhwaff - 54798433

29. fbfuadsh - 31304265
    gzfuwzsb - 57300671
    bashhgag - 14699535

Questions 30-35.

DIRECTIONS: Questions 30 through 35 are to be answered on the basis of the information in the Weekly Requisition Form below.

WEEKLY REQUISITION FORM

Storehouse 17	Date 7.17	Dept. Code 809	Dept. Budget Code 13942	Dept. Requisition No. 1029		
Deliver to: Requisition Dept. Atlantic Hospital			Unit and/or Division Kitchen	Address 66 W. Highland Blvd.		
Storehouse Item Code	Description Incl. Size, Number or Measurements		Unit of Issue	No. Units Requested	Unit Price	Tot. Cost
895	Chocolate Syrup #10 can		case	5	7.35	
1926	Mayonnaise 1 gal. jar		case	2	6.73	13.46
1945	Black pepper, ground 1.lb. can		lb	3		1.89
1976	34 fresh eggs			7	.41	2.87
220	Pineapple, crushed #10 can		case	4	5.89	23.56
5395	Straws 8 1/2" long 500 to box		box	12	.47	5.64
452	Applesauce 4 1/2 oz. jar 24/case		case		1.65	6.60
Requested By John Smith	Title Shop Clerk	Material Issued By _____ Date _____		Material Received By Signed _____ Date _____		
Approved By	Supervisor	Total No. Pieces ___		Total No. Pieces ___		

30. What is the total cost of the chocolate syrup order described in the requisition form above?

    A. $36.75   B. $34.35   C. $31.65   D. $30.15

31. The week of 7/24, the price of a gallon jar of mayonnaise increased by 4 cents. If there are 6 gallon jars of mayonnaise per case, how much is the total cost of the mayonnaise order for the week of 7/24, if the order quantity is the same as the previous week?

    A. $6.97   B. $7.21   C. $13.68   D. $13.94

32. What is the unit price for ground black pepper as described in the requisition form above?

    A. 36¢   B. 43¢   C. 57¢   D. 63¢

33. Based on the information provided in the requisition form above, what is the correct unit of issue for fresh eggs?

    A. Each   B. Container   C. Dozen   D. Case

34. There are 6 #10 cans of crushed pineapple per case. Based on the information in the requisition form above, how many #10 cans of pineapple are being ordered?

    A. 16   B. 20   C. 24   D. 30

35. Each week the cook at Atlantic Hospital uses 84 4 1/2 ounce jars of applesauce. Based on the requisition for the week of 7/17, how many cases must be ordered to fill the need for the following week (7/24) in order to avoid storing an excess supply of applesauce? (Assume that there was no excess from the week previous to 7/17.)   35._____

   A. 1   B. 2   C. 3   D. 4

36. Suppose that the shop in which you worked received 421 pieces of mail in one month, of which 64 were requests for information.   36._____
   The percent of letters which were requests for information is MOST NEARLY

   A. 13.2%   B. 15.2%   C. 15.5%   D. 16.1%

37. The following is the year's stock issue record of cans of oil distributed for use in Agency Y: January - 107; February - 94; March - 113; April - 118; May - 122; June - 87; July - 89; August - 98; September - 110; October - 101; November - 105; December - 106.   37._____
   The monthly average of cans of oil distributed is MOST NEARLY

   A. 100   B. 102   C. 104   D. 106

38. Two trucks, A and B, are carrying stock from a warehouse to the shop. The weight of the truck alone is the tare; the weight of the loaded truck is the gross weight. Truck A has a tare of 4,637 pounds, and a gross weight of 6,955 pounds. Truck B has a tare of 4,489 pounds, and a gross weight of 6,723 pounds.   38._____
   What is the total weight of the loads of both trucks?
   _____ pounds.

   A. 3,452   B. 3,564   C. 4,552   D. 4,653

39. A stock carton measures 24" long, 18" wide, and 24" high. What is the maximum number of boxes measuring 4 1/2" long, 3" wide, and 3" high that can be packed inside the carton?   39._____

   A. 135   B. 256   C. 405   D. 432

40. If a ream of paper weighs 11 ounces, 36 reams of paper will weigh_____ pounds, _____ ounces.   40._____

   A. 22; 8   B. 24; 12   C. 33; 0   D. 39; 6

KEY (CORRECT ANSWERS)

1.	C	11.	A	21.	C	31.	D
2.	B	12.	C	22.	B	32.	D
3.	B	13.	C	23.	D	33.	C
4.	B	14.	A	24.	C	34.	C
5.	A	15.	A	25.	C	35.	C
6.	C	16.	C	26.	B	36.	B
7.	B	17.	A	27.	B	37.	C
8.	B	18.	A	28.	D	38.	C
9.	C	19.	A	29.	C	39.	B
10.	B	20.	A	30.	A	40.	B

TEST 2

DIRECTIONS: Each question or incomplete statement is followed by several suggested answers or completions. Select the one that BEST answers the question or completes the statement. *PRINT THE LETTER OF THE CORRECT ANSWER IN THE SPACE AT THE RIGHT.*

Questions 1-6.

DIRECTIONS: Questions 1 through 6 are to be answered on the basis of the information below.

A certain shop keeps an informational card file for all suppliers and merchandise. On each card is the supplier's name, the contract number for the merchandise he supplies, and a delivery date for the merchandise. In this filing system, the supplier's name is filed alphabetically, the contract number for the merchandise is filed numerically, and the delivery date is filed chronologically.

In Questions 1 through 6, there are five notations numbered 1 through 5 shown in Column I. Each notation is made up of a supplier's name, a contract number, and a date and is to be filed according to the following rules:

First: File in alphabetical order
Second: When two or more notations have the same supplier, file according to the contract number in numerical order beginning with the lowest number
Third: When two or more notations have the same supplier and contract number, file according to the date beginning with the earliest date

In Column II, the numbers 1 through 5 are arranged in four ways to show different possible orders in which the merchandise information might be filed. Pick the answer (A, B, C, or D) in Column II in which the notations are arranged according to the above filing rules.

SAMPLE QUESTION:

Column I
1. Cluney (4865) 6/17/72
2. Roster (2466) 5/10/71
3. Altool (7114) 10/15/72
4. Cluney (5276) 12/18/71
5. Cluney (4865) 4/8/72

Column II
A. 2, 3, 4, 1, 5
B. 2, 5, 1, 3, 4
C. 3, 2, 1, 4, 5
D. 3, 5, 1, 4, 2

The correct way to file the notations is:
(3) Altool (7114) 10/15/72
(5) Cluney (4865) 4/8/72
(1) Cluney (4865) 6/17/72
(4) Cluney (5276) 12/18/71
(2) Roster (2466) 5/10/71

Since the correct filing order is 3, 5, 1, 4, 2, the answer to the sample question is D.

19

	Column I		Column II

1.
   1. Fenten (38511) 1/4/73
   2. Meadowlane (5020) 11/1/72
   3. Whitehall (36142) 6/22/72
   4. Clinton (4141) 5/26/71
   5. Mester (8006) 4/20/71

   A. 3, 5, 2, 1, 4
   B. 4, 1, 2, 5, 3
   C. 4, 2, 5, 3, 1
   D. 5, 4, 3, 1, 2

   1.___

2.
   1. Harvard (2286) 2/19/70
   2. Parker (1781) 4/12/72
   3. Lenson (9044) 6/6/72
   4. Brothers (38380) 10/11/72
   5. Parker (41400) 12/20/70

   A. 2, 4, 3, 1, 5
   B. 2, 1, 3, 4, 5
   C. 4, 1, 3, 2, 5
   D. 5, 2, 3, 1, 4

   2.___

3.
   1. Newtone (3197) 8/22/70
   2. Merritt (4071) 8/8/72
   3. Writebest (60666) 4/7/71
   4. Maltons (34380) 3/30/72
   5. Merrit (4071) 7/16/71

   A. 1, 4, 2, 5, 3
   B. 4, 2, 1, 5, 3
   C. 4, 5, 2, 1, 3
   D. 5, 2, 4, 3, 1

   3.___

4.
   1. Weinburt (45514) 6/4/71
   2. Owntye (35860) 10/4/72
   3. Weinburt (45515) 2/1/72
   4. Fasttex (7677) 11/10/71
   5. Owntye (4574) 7/17/72

   A. 4, 5, 2, 1, 3
   B. 4, 2, 5, 3, 1
   C. 4, 2, 5, 1, 3
   D. 4, 5, 2, 3, 1

   4.___

5.
   1. Premier (1003) 7/29/70
   2. Phylson (0031) 5/5/72
   3. Lathen (3328) 10/3/71
   4. Harper (8046) 8/18/72
   5. Lathen (3328) 12/1/72

   A. 2, 1, 4, 3, 5
   B. 3, 5, 4, 1, 2
   C. 4, 1, 2, 3, 5
   D. 4, 3, 5, 2, 1

   5.___

6.
   1. Repper (46071) 10/14/72
   2. Destex (77271) 8/27/72
   3. Clawson (30736) 7/28/71
   4. Destex (27207) 8/17/71
   5. Destex (77271) 4/14/71

   A. 3, 2, 4, 5, 1
   B. 3, 4, 2, 5, 1
   C. 3, 4, 5, 2, 1
   D. 3, 5, 4, 2, 1

   6.___

7. Assume that a clerk is asked to prepare a special report which he has not prepared before. He decides to make a written outline of the report before writing it in full. This decision by the clerk is

   A. *good,* mainly because it helps the writer to organize his thoughts and decide what will go into the report
   B. *good,* mainly because it clearly shows the number of topics, number of pages, and the length of the report
   C. *poor,* mainly because it wastes the time of the writer since he will have to write the full report anyway
   D. *poor,* mainly because it confines the writer to those areas listed in the outline

   7.___

8. Assume that a clerk in the water resources central shop is asked to prepare an important report, giving the location and condition of various fire hydrants in the city. One of the hydrants in question is broken and is spewing rusty water in the street, creating a flooded condition in the area. The clerk reports that the hydrant is broken but does not report the escaping water or the flood.
Of the following, the BEST evaluation of the clerk's decision about what to report is that it is basically

    A. *correct,* chiefly because a lengthy report would contain irrelevant information
    B. *correct,* chiefly because a more detailed description of a hydrant should be made by a fireman, not a clerk
    C. *incorrect,* chiefly because the clerk's assignment was to describe the condition of the hydrant and he should give a full explanation
    D. *incorrect,* chiefly because the clerk should include as much information as possible in his report whether or not it is relevant

8._____

Questions 9-14.

DIRECTIONS: Questions 9 through 14 are to be answered ONLY on the information contained in the following chart, which shows the number of requisitions filled by Storeroom A during each month of the year.

NUMBER OF REQUISITIONS HANDLED EACH MONTH
DURING THE YEAR BY STOREROOM A

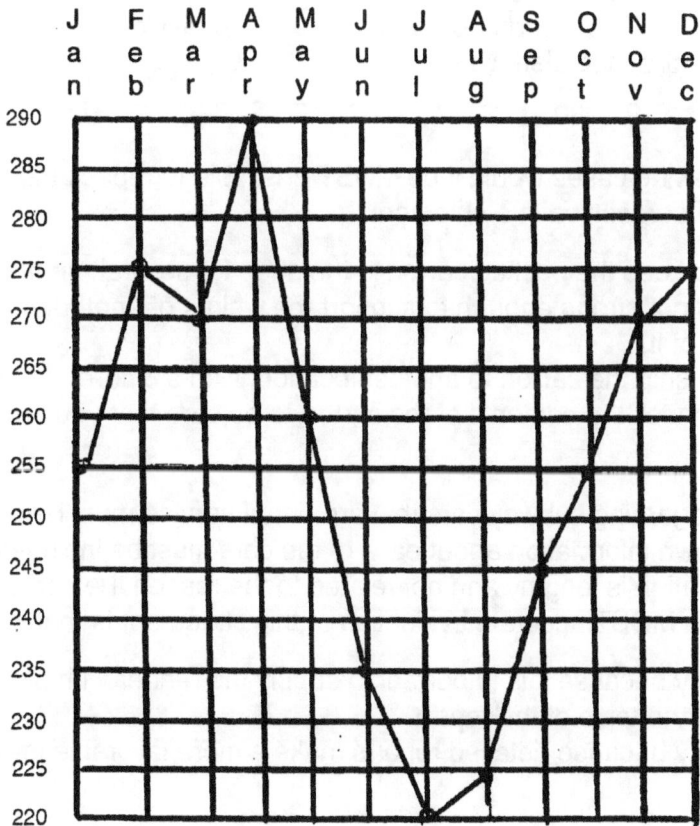

9. According to the above chart, the average number of requisitions handled per month by Storeroom A during the first six months of the year is MOST NEARLY

   A. 250 B. 260 C. 270 D. 280

10. It is expected that the number of requisitions Storeroom A will handle next year will be 10 percent more than it handled this year.
    The number of requisitions Storeroom A is expected to handle next year will MOST likely be

    A. 2,763 B. 3,070 C. 3,382 D. 3,440

11. The month during which the number of requisitions handled showed the GREATEST decrease from the previous month was

    A. April B. May C. June D. July

12. During May there were 3 clerks assigned to Storeroom A. One man went on vacation for the month of June and was not replaced.
    The number of additional orders handled by each man working in June over the number of orders handled per man in May was MOST NEARLY

    A. 20 B. 27 C. 32 D. 36

13. During June, July, and August, 8 percent of the requisitions handled were rush orders. The number of rush orders handled during these three months is MOST NEARLY

    A. 55 B. 60 C. 65 D. 70

14. During November, there were three clerks assigned to Storeroom A.
    If one handled 95 requisitions and another handled 85 requisitions, the number of requisitions handled by the third clerk was

    A. 70 B. 80 C. 90 D. 100

15. In which of the following cases would it be MOST desirable to repack the contents of a carton which was just received in a shipment?

    A. You expect to keep the packed carton in the shop for several months.
    B. The carton is not strong enough to support the weight of another carton you want to put on top of it.
    C. You intend to ship the carton to another location, with a different address.
    D. You want to check the contents of the carton to be sure that you received the correct shipment.

16. The daily reports regarding subway cars that are out of service must be prepared in great detail. All known information about each of the cars must be included in the report, even if such information is lengthy and not related to the reason the car is out of service.
    Of the following, the MOST accurate evaluation of this statement is that it is basically

    A. *correct*, mainly because it is important to supply the reader with background information about the topic of the report
    B. *correct*, mainly because detailed reports make a more favorable impression upon the reader

C. *incorrect,* mainly because a good report should be as brief as possible and contain only relevant information
D. *incorrect,* mainly because background information about each car should be supplied in a separate report

Questions 17-22.

DIRECTIONS: Questions 17 through 22 are to be answered ONLY on the basis of the information in the chart below.

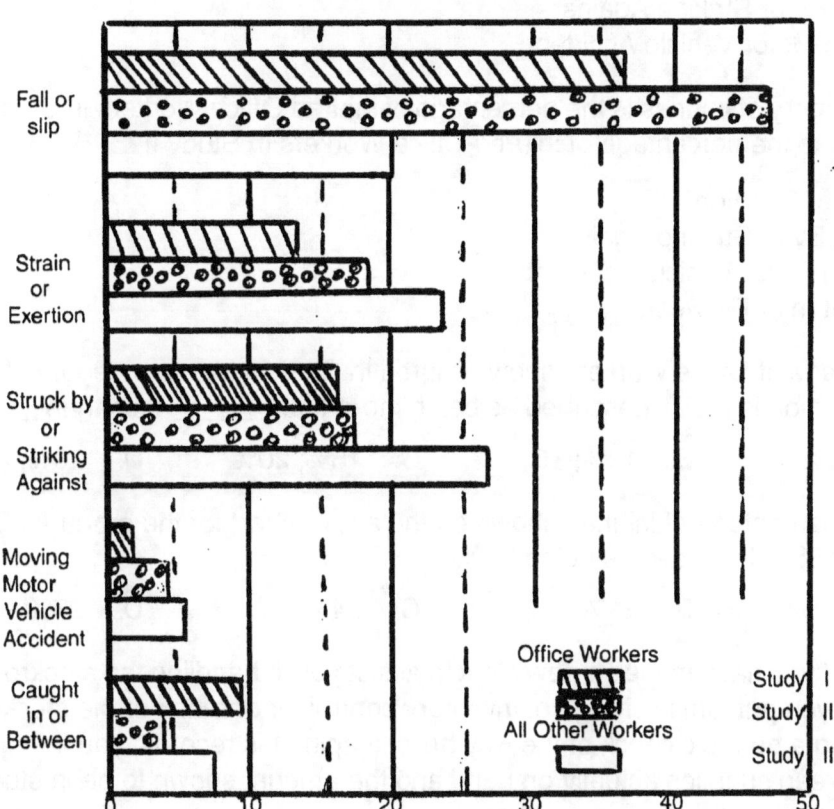

LEADING ACCIDENT TYPES
Office Employees Compared With Other Injured Workers

The above chart shows the results of two studies concerning injuries to office workers. Study I was done only for office workers. The results are represented by ▨ , Study II compared injuries to office workers with injuries to all other workers. In Study II, office workers are represented by ▦ ; all other workers by ☐

17. In Study II, in which category of accident was there a 5% difference between the percentage of Office Workers injured and the percentage of All Other Workers injured?

    A. Strain or Exertion
    B. Struck by or Striking Against
    C. Moving Motor Vehicle Accident
    D. Caught In or Between

18. In which category of accident is the average percentage of all Office Workers injured closest to the percentage of injuries for All Other Workers?

    A. Fall or Slip
    B. Strain or Exertion
    C. Struck By or Striking Against
    D. Caught In or Between

18.____

19. In which category is the percentage of All Other Workers injured MOST NEARLY one-half of the average percentage for all Office Workers injured?

    A. Fall or Slip
    B. Strain or Exertion
    C. Struck By or Striking Against
    D. Moving Motor Vehicle Accident

19.____

20. In which category of injuries is the percentage of injured Office Workers in Study I shown to be closest to the percentage of injured Office Workers in Study II?

    A. Strain or Exertion
    B. Struck By or Striking Against
    C. Moving Motor Vehicle Accident
    D. Caught In or Between

20.____

21. The percentage of Office Workers shown injured in Study II for the category of accident Strain or Exertion is BEST described as being more than _____ less than _____ .

    A. 5%; 10%   B. 10%; 15%   C. 15%; 20%   D. 20%; 24%

21.____

22. The largest percentage of injuries shown on the above chart for the group All Other Workers is BEST described as being MOST NEARLY

    A. 18%   B. 21%   C. 24%   D. 27%

22.____

23. Suppose that you have trained a new clerk to assist you in handling the stockroom. A few weeks later, you put him in charge of inventory control for one-half of the stockroom. When making a periodic check of the way he is keeping his records, you find quite a difference between supplies actually on hand and the amount shown to be in stock on the inventory record cards.
    Of the following, the BEST action to take in this situation is to

    A. report the clerk to your supervisor because he is not keeping the records properly
    B. tell the clerk that you will order an additional supply of the items to cover the difference
    C. review the inventory control procedure with the clerk in order to locate the source of the error
    D. advise the clerk that he is not suited for this job and that you will recommend that he be transferred

23.____

24. You are the clerk in charge of the time cards on which the men in the shop sign in in the mornings and sign out in the afternoons. Suppose that one day a co-worker with whom you are especially friendly asks you to let him sign 15 minutes before the others so that he can get a seat on the subway.
    Of the following, which is the MOST desirable action to take?

24.____

A. Go on and let your friend sign out; no one will know about it except the two of you
B. Tell your friend you'll let him sign out this first time, but warn him not to ask again
C. Tell your friend you are going to report him to your supervisor and to his, so he will not try anything like this again
D. Explain to your friend that this is a violation of the rules and that, even though you're friends, you cannot grant his request

25. Suppose that one of the road crew working in a shop receives a great many personal phone calls and constantly requests the clerk to take detailed messages for him. Taking these messages is beginning to take up a lot of the clerk's time.
The BEST thing for the clerk to do under the circumstances is to

    A. tell the man's supervisor that he should put a stop to his men receiving so many personal phone calls
    B. purposely omit or confuse some messages so the worker will stop requesting that he take them
    C. explain to the worker that he cannot spend so much time taking messages because it is interfering with his work
    D. continue to take the messages, but write a report to the worker's supervisor complaining about the phone calls

26. For a six-month period including the previous months, 6 additional mechanics are assigned to work in a shop for a special assignment. The clerk must prepare a vacation schedule for all the men in the shop based on the men's requests and their seniority in the department. Several of the 12 *regulars* in the shop believe they should be given priority, and ask the clerk to do so, even though some of the other men have greater seniority.
Under the circumstances, the clerk should

    A. immediately report the *regulars* to their supervisor for trying to break the rules
    B. tell them that, since all the men are assigned to the shop, he must make up the schedule as if they were all *regulars*
    C. try to satisfy the *regulars* since they will be around as co-workers after the other 6 men leave
    D. tell the new men that some of the *regulars* are trying to make trouble for them

27. Assume that you receive a written complaint from an irate vendor shortly after your supervisor has begun his vacation. The supervisor is not expected back for several weeks. The complaint is complex, and you are uncertain about how to reply to it.
Of the following, the BEST course of action for you to take in this situation is to

    A. answer the vendor's complaint as well as you can
    B. assign a clerk in your shop to reply to the vendor's complaint
    C. wait until your supervisor returns from vacation
    D. write to the vendor to tell him that the complaint has been received and that your office is looking into it

28. Suppose that you are a clerk in a transit authority repair shop. A member of the public has called the transit authority to complain about poor ventilation in a subway car, and the call has been transferred to your office. The man demands to speak to the foreman, who is gone for the day to attend a meeting. The man becomes increasingly angry and abusive when you tell him the foreman has gone.
Under the circumstances, the BEST thing for you to do is to

A. tell the man that if he continues to yell at you you will hang up
B. try to calm the man down and then tell him you will record his complaint and report it to the foreman
C. speak to the man as loudly and rudely as he is speaking to you until he calms down
D. hang up the telephone since the man is not rational and there is no point in talking to him

29. You and a co-worker are both asked by your supervisor to work on a job that requires two men working full-time to complete it on time. You find that your co-worker is *goofing off* and not doing his share of the work.
Of the following, the FIRST thing you should do is to

A. try to do enough work for two of you, so the job will be finished on time
B. begin to goof off also, so your co-worker will not think he can take advantage of you
C. tell your co-worker that you think he is not doing his share, and that you will have to go to the supervisor if he doesn't straighten out
D. report your co-worker to your supervisor, and tell the supervisor you refuse to continue unless he assigns someone else to work with you

Questions 30-33.

DIRECTIONS: Questions 30 through 33 are to be answered on the basis of the information in the report below.

To: Chief, Division X
From: Mrs. Helen Jones, Clerk
Subject: Accident Involving Two Employees, Mr. John Smith and Mr. Robert Brown

On February 15, Mr. Smith and Mr. Brown were both injured in an accident occurring in the shop at 10 Long Road. No one was in the area of the accident other than Mr. Smith and Mr. Brown. Both of these employees described the following circumstances:

1. Mr. Brown saw the largest tool on the wall begin to fall from where it was hanging and ran up to push Mr. Smith out of the way and to prevent the tool from falling, if possible.
2. Mr. Smith was standing near the wall under some tools which were hanging on nails in the wall.
3. Mr. Brown was standing a few steps from the wall.
4. Mr. Brown stepped toward Mr. Smith, who was on the floor and away from the falling tool. He tripped and fell over a piece of equipment on the floor.
5. Mr. Brown pushed Mr. Smith who slipped on some grease on the floor and fell to the side, out of the way of the falling tool.
6. Mr. Brown tried to avoid Mr. Smith as he fell. In so doing, he fell against some pipes which were leaning against the wall. The pipes fell on both Mr. Brown and Mr. Smith.

Mr. Smith and Mr. Brown were both badly bruised and shaken. They were sent to the General Hospital to determine if any bones were broken. The office was later notified that neither employee was seriously hurt.

Since the accident, matters relating to safety and accident prevention around the shop have occupied the staff. There have been a number of complaints about the location of tools and equipment. Several employees are reluctant to work in the shop unless conditions are improved. Please advise as to the best way to handle this situation.

30. The one of the following which it is MOST important to add to the above memorandum is

    A. a signature line
    B. a transmittal note
    C. the date of the memo
    D. the initials of the typist

31. The MOST logical order in which to list the circumstances relative to the accident is

    A. as shown (1, 2, 3, 4, 5, 6)
    B. 2, 3, 1, 5, 4, 6
    C. 1, 5, 4, 6, 3, 2
    D. 3, 2, 4, 6, 1, 5

32. The one of the following which does NOT properly belong with the rest of the memorandum is

    A. the first section of paragraph 1
    B. the list of circumstances
    C. paragraph 2
    D. paragraph 3

33. According to the information in the memorandum, the BEST description of the subject is

    A. effect of accident on work output of the division
    B. description of accident involving Mr. Smith and Mr. Brown
    C. recommendations on how to avoid future accidents
    D. safety and accident control in the shop

34. The items of stock which should usually be issued FIRST are those which

    A. are of best quality
    B. are of poorest quality
    C. have been longest in the storeroom
    D. are not being stored any more

35. If all the new stock of a certain item will not fit on the shelf where the old stock is stored, it would usually be BEST to

    A. store some of the stock in a new location
    B. store the excess stock in the aisle near the shelf
    C. keep the new stock in the receiving area until the old stock is issued
    D. move all the stock to a new location

36. The MAJOR purpose of maintaining an adequate inventory is to 36.____

   A. prevent supply shortages
   B. reduce waste of storage space
   C. increase the dollar value of the organization
   D. provide enough jobs for stockmen

37. The term *This Side Up* is MOST appropriate on a carton containing 37.____

   A. canned food   B. boxes of paper clips
   C. clothing   D. a typewriter

38. Storeroom records are essential in order to have a supply of each stock item always 38.____
   available.
   What information is it NOT necessary to include in storeroom records?

   A. When to reorder stock items
   B. Required delivery time
   C. Means of transportation of delivery
   D. Sources of stock supply

39. Assume that you usually order a new supply of tires for your agency's fleet of trucks 39.____
   every 6 months. Just before you place an order, you find out that there is a 10% increase
   expected in the price of tires during the next 3 months.
   Of the following, the BEST action for you to take FIRST is to

   A. automatically order a double supply of tires before the prices are increased in order
      to save the 10%
   B. ignore the expected price increase because it is only expected, not definite
   C. determine what the storage and other costs for an extra order of tires will be and
      compare it with the cost of a 10% price increase
   D. wait until the new prices go into effect because the more expensive tires will proba-
      bly be better quality

40. Assume that your supervisor asks you to do a certain job of unpacking cartons. He tells 40.____
   you how to do it, but you believe there is a better, faster way.
   The MOST advisable course of action for you to take is to

   A. follow your supervisor's orders and unpack the cartons his way, without comment
   B. unpack the cartons your way and then show your supervisor the result
   C. ask your co-workers which way they think is better, and do the job that way
   D. explain your way to your supervisor and then ask him which method you should
      use

KEY (CORRECT ANSWERS)

1.	B	11.	B	21.	C	31.	B
2.	C	12.	C	22.	D	32.	D
3.	C	13.	A	23.	C	33.	B
4.	A	14.	C	24.	D	34.	C
5.	D	15.	B	25.	C	35.	A
6.	C	16.	C	26.	B	36.	A
7.	A	17.	A	27.	D	37.	D
8.	C	18.	D	28.	B	38.	C
9.	B	19.	A	29.	C	39.	C
10.	C	20.	B	30.	C	40.	D

EXAMINATION SECTION
TEST 1

DIRECTIONS: Each question or incomplete statement is followed by several suggested answers or completions. Select the one that BEST answers the question or completes the statement. *PRINT THE LETTER OF THE CORRECT ANSWER IN THE SPACE AT THE RIGHT.*

1. The stock items on the purchase order should be the same as those on the shipment receipt at time of delivery.
   In general, it is BEST to check this at the time that the stock items are

   A. received in the storehouse
   B. ordered by the agency using the material
   C. issued by the storehouse personnel
   D. certified for payment

   1.____

2. Sawdust and shredded paper are materials that are generally used in which one of the following operations?

   A. Packing
   B. Inventory
   C. Spraying
   D. Transporting

   2.____

3. Storage areas with good air circulation and ventilation are generally considered

   A. *good,* only in hot and humid weather
   B. *good,* to retard mold growth
   C. *poor,* due to danger of fire
   D. *poor,* because of cleaning costs

   3.____

4. To get the best use from storage areas, it is usually BEST to use high ceilinged areas for storing

   A. heavy, bulky stock items
   B. lightweight stock items
   C. loose stock items in small bins
   D. extremely large-sized stock items

   4.____

5. The section of the storeroom that can carry the least weight should generally NOT be used for storing stock items that

   A. have a large size
   B. have a small size
   C. are very heavy
   D. are very light

   5.____

6. Where should you store unusually large and heavy stock items that are used very often?

   A. As close to the shipping and receiving areas as possible
   B. Away from work areas, such as shipping and receiving
   C. On hand trucks until the using agency asks for the item
   D. Only in storage areas which are outside the storehouse

   6.____

7. Which of the following would be MOST important in deciding how wide the space should be between cartons stacked in a storage area?

   7.____

31

A. Type of equipment that will be used to handle the stock
B. Size of the storage area
C. Number of employees in the storage area
D. How far the storage area is away from the receiving area

8. Stock items that might break, chip, or be crushed should be packed 8.____

   A. *tightly* with items touching each other
   B. *loosely* in a heavy wood container
   C. *tightly* with little movement allowed between items
   D. *tightly* with cushioning material between items

9. Suppose that some stock items delivered by truck are found to be damaged before they are unloaded. 9.____
   Which of the following actions would be BEST to take?

   A. Take the damaged stock and then give it out first to prevent further damage
   B. Refuse to take any damaged items
   C. Tell the driver of the truck to return the entire shipment
   D. Tell your supervisor about the damage so that he can take the necessary steps

10. It is dangerous to store gasoline because 10.____

    A. it can only be stored in specially constructed rooms in a storehouse
    B. it gives off vapors that can easily burn
    C. it can explode when moved around
    D. no one has found a safe way of storing gasoline

11. Gases are usually stored under pressure in steel cans. Which of the following is the LEAST dangerous practice? 11.____

    A. Allowing the cans to come in contact with electrical circuits
    B. Lifting the cans by their valves
    C. Allowing the cans to touch each other
    D. Keeping the valves on the cans open after the gas has been used up

12. Acids are a danger in storage because leakage may result in a sudden fire if contact is made with other chemicals. When storing acids, the one of the following practices which is INCORRECT is to 12.____

    A. keep them in heavy duty metal cans
    B. store them in isolated areas
    C. protect the containers against breakage
    D. keep flames or lit matches out of areas where acids are stored

13. Tape with a cellophane backing will become wrinkled and lumpy if stored in an area that is 13.____

    A. warm   B. cool   C. damp   D. very dry

14. To keep wooden furniture from warping and twisting, it should be stored in an area that is 14.____

    A. warm and dry   B. warm and damp
    C. cool and dry   D. cool and damp

15. Which one of the following items should NOT be stored in a very dry storage area? 15.____

    A. Soup cubes B. Baking soda
    C. Tea leaves D. Lettuce

16. Some food items can easily spoil. 16.____
    If they are packed in torn sacks or broken boxes, they should be stored

    A. in exactly the same way as other items
    B. just after fixing the sacks or boxes
    C. inside a bin in the storage area
    D. after spraying with DDT or another insect spray

17. Of the following items, which one is MOST likely to be damaged by insects? 17.____

    A. Iron pipes B. Rubber inner tubes
    C. Plastic tubing D. Grain products

18. Which one of the following items, when stored properly, has the SHORTEST storage life? 18.____

    A. Baked products B. Noodles
    C. Cornstarch D. Rolled oats

19. Which one of the following food items is LEAST likely to give off smells in a storehouse? 19.____

    A. Cheese B. Onions
    C. Fresh peaches D. Baking powder

20. The word *inventory* means the practice of counting all the stock items within each class 20.____
    of items.
    However, before an inventory can be done,

    A. the stock items must be thoroughly cleaned
    B. all stock items must be located and identified
    C. old stock items should be thrown away
    D. stock items that have been returned by the user should not be counted

---

KEY (CORRECT ANSWERS)

1. A   11. C
2. A   12. A
3. B   13. C
4. B   14. C
5. C   15. D

6. A   16. B
7. A   17. D
8. D   18. A
9. D   19. D
10. B   20. B

TEST 2

DIRECTIONS: Each question or incomplete statement is followed by several suggested answers or completions. Select the one that BEST answers the question or completes the statement. *PRINT THE LETTER OF THE CORRECT ANSWER IN THE SPACE AT THE RIGHT.*

1. *Pliers* may BEST be classified under 1.____
   - A. food products
   - B. tools
   - C. office supplies
   - D. machinery

2. *White pine lumber* may BEST be classified under 2.____
   - A. building materials
   - B. laboratory materials
   - C. safety materials
   - D. seeds and plants

3. *Linseed oil* may BEST be classified under 3.____
   - A. drugs and chemicals
   - B. painters' supplies
   - C. building materials
   - D. fuel and fuel oils

4. *Ceiling tiles* may BEST be classified under 4.____
   - A. office supplies
   - B. hardware
   - C. electrical supplies
   - D. building materials

5. *Floor finish remover* may BEST be classified under 5.____
   - A. insecticides
   - B. drugs
   - C. machinery
   - D. cleaning supplies

6. *Arm slings* may BEST be classified under 6.____
   - A. hospital supplies
   - B. clothing
   - C. school supplies
   - D. office supplies

7. *Staplers* may BEST be classified under 7.____
   - A. office supplies
   - B. laboratory supplies
   - C. machinery and metals
   - D. engineering supplies

8. *Canvas stretcher* may BEST be classified under 8.____
   - A. laboratory apparatus
   - B. hospital supplies
   - C. clothing
   - D. tools

9. *Switches* may BEST be classified under 9.____
   - A. camera supplies
   - B. vehicles
   - C. electrical supplies
   - D. pipes and pipe fittings

10. *Bandages* may BEST be classified under 10.____
    - A. laboratory equipment
    - B. surgical instruments
    - C. hospital supplies
    - D. hose and belting

Questions 11-15.

DIRECTIONS: Questions 11 through 15 are to be answered on the basis of the information given below.

LISTING OF PAPER
FOUND IN STOCKROOM A, ON APRIL 30

	Quantity Ordered by Stockroom A (in dozen reams)	Quantity in Stock Before Delivery (in dozen reams)	Cost Per Ream	Location of Stock in Stockroom
8 1/2"x11" Blue	17	5	$0.94	Bin A7
8 1/2"x11" Buff	8	3	$0.93	Bin A7
8 1/2"x11" Green	11	4	$0.95	Bin B4
8 1/2"x11" Pink	10	4	$0.93	Bin B4
8 1/2"x11" White	80	15	$0.86	Bin A8
8 1/2"x13" White	76	12	$1.02	Bin A8
8 1/2"x14" Blue	7	2	$1.19	Bin A7
8 1/2"x14" Buff	7	3	$1.18	Bin A7
8 1/2"x14" Green	5	2	$1.20	Bin B4
8 1/2"x14" Pink	8	4	$1.18	Bin B4
8 1/2"x14" White	110	28	$1.15	Bin A8
8 1/2"x14" Yellow	2	1	$1.23	Bin C6

11. How many reams of 8 1/2"x13" paper will there be in stock if only one-half of the amount ordered is delivered? _____ reams.   11.____

    A. 456   B. 600   C. 912   D. 1056

12. Suppose all ordered material is delivered.   12.____
    The bin that will have the MOST reams of paper is

    A. A7   B. A8   C. B4   D. C6

13. Suppose all ordered material has been delivered.   13.____
    What is the approximate value of all 8 1/2"x11" paper which is in Bin B4?

    A. $27   B. $171   C. $198   D. $327

14. How many reams of white paper of all sizes were ordered? _____ reams.   14.____

    A. 55   B. 266   C. 660   D. 3192

15. Before any of the orders were delivered, the following requests were filled and removed   15.____
    from the stockroom:
    2 dozen reams 8 1/2"x11" Blue; 2 dozen reams 8 1/2"x11" Green;
    7 dozen reams 8 1/2"x11" White; 5 dozen reams 8 1/2"x13" White;
    1 dozen reams 8 1/2"x14" Green; 13 dozen reams 8 1/2"x14" White.
    How many reams of paper were left in the stockroom after the above requests were filled?

    A. 30   B. 53   C. 636   D. 996

Questions 16-20.

DIRECTIONS: Questions 16 through 20 are to be answered SOLELY on the basis of the information given in the table below.

CONTROLLED DRUG A

Time Period	Purchase Order Number	Quantity Ordered	*Quantity Delivered by Vendor	Quantity Distributed during 2-week Period	Inventory Balance end of 2-Week Period
April 23-May 6	110,327	105 ounces	135 ounces	27 ounces	108 ounces
May 7-May 20	111,437	42 ounces	40 ounces	39 ounces	109 ounces
May 21-June 3	112,347	37 ounces	27 ounces	32 ounces	104 ounces
June 4-June 17	112,473	35 ounces	35 ounces	45 ounces	94 ounces
June 18-July 1	114,029	40 ounces	40 ounces	37 ounces	97 ounces

*Delivery is made on first day of time period.

16. The *difference* between Quantity Ordered and Quantity Delivered was greatest on Purchase Order Number

    A. 110,327   B. 111,437   C. 112,347   D. 112,473

17. The *difference* between the total number of ounces ordered and the total number of ounces delivered on April 23 through June 18 is _____ ounces.

    A. 17   B. 18   C. 19   D. 20

18. Suppose that average weekly usage was expected to be 26 ounces per week. Your supervisor has asked you to tell him whenever inventory balances get below a four-week level.
    Under these conditions, you should have told your supervisor during the two-week period beginning

    A. April 23, May 21, June 4, June 18
    B. May 21, June 4, June 18
    C. May 21, June 18
    D. June 4, June 18

19. The GREATEST decreases in inventory balances happened between the two-week periods beginning

    A. April 23 and May 7   B. May 7 and May 21
    C. May 21 and June 4   D. June 4 and June 18

20. Suppose a new program has been started at your hospital and the weekly usage of Drug   20._____
    A is expected to be 52 ounces per week.
    If your supervisor must keep on hand a four-week supply, then the amount that should
    be delivered for the two-week period beginning on July 2 is _____ ounces.
    A. 52   B. 111   C. 208   D. 211

KEY (CORRECT ANSWERS)

1. B   11. B
2. A   12. B
3. B   13. D
4. D   14. D
5. D   15. C

6. A   16. A
7. A   17. B
8. B   18. D
9. C   19. C
10. C   20. B

TEST 3

DIRECTIONS: Each question or incomplete statement is followed by several suggested answers or completions. Select the one that BEST answers the question or completes the statement. *PRINT THE LETTER OF THE CORRECT ANSWER IN THE SPACE AT THE RIGHT.*

1. Suppose that 3-foot high boxes are to be stacked in one pile on a 4-inch platform. In addition, 4-inch thick separators are placed between each layer of boxes. Suppose that the ceiling is 22 feet high, and there must be at least 1 1/2 feet of space between the ceiling and the stacked boxes.
   What is the GREATEST number of boxes that can be stacked?

   A. 4   B. 5   C. 6   D. 7   1.____

2. A part of a storeroom measures 14 1/2 feet by 6 1/4 feet.   2.____
   The number of square feet in this part is _____ square feet.

   A. 8 1/4   B. 20 3/4   C. 90 5/8   D. 94 3/4

3. How many *cubic* feet of storage space would be taken up by 20 boxes, when each box 3.____
   measures 2 feet high, 2 feet wide, and 3 feet long? _____ cubic feet.

   A. 12   B. 27   C. 140   D. 240

4. Suppose that a truckload of canned items has been unloaded. There are six rows of 4.____
   boxes with seven boxes in each row. Each box has two dozen cans in it.
   How many cans are there all together?

   A. 24   B. 144   C. 510   D. 1008

5. Suppose that the average weekly use of tissue amounts to 180 rolls.   5.____
   At least how many boxes must be ordered for a 4-week period if there are 144 rolls in each box?

   A. 2   B. 3   C. 4   D. 5

6. Suppose that a stockroom started the week with an initial supply of 3 gross of pencils 6.____
   and that one gross equals 144 pencils. After orders were filled, the stockroom had an inventory at the end of the week as follows: 2 gross of 4H pencils; 3 dozen 2B pencils; 1 1/2 dozen HB pencils; and 15H pencils.
   How many pencils were ordered?
   _____ pencils.

   A. 22   B. 45   C. 75   D. 97

7. How many 18-inch pieces can be cut from 10 lengths of 8-foot glass tubing?   7.____
   _____ pieces.

   A. 47   B. 50   C. 53   D. 56

8. Suppose a roll of wire is 27 feet 3 inches long. A piece of wire measuring 18 feet 9 inches 8.____
   in length is cut from the roll.
   What is the length of wire left on the roll? _____ feet _____ inches.

   A. 7; 3   B. 7; 6   C. 8; 3   D. 8; 6

38

9. Suppose that 25% of a delivery of canned peaches was spoiled.
   If 36 cans were spoiled, then the delivery had a total of _____ cans.
   A. 9   B. 25   C. 144   D. 180

10. Suppose that a one-quart can of white flat ceiling paint weighs 5 pounds.
    What is the GREATEST number of quart cans that can be stored on a shelf that supports 167 pounds?
    _____ quart cans.
    A. 5   B. 33   C. 41   D. 67

11. Assume that the following orders were filled from a 55-gallon drum of oil: 9 pints, 7 pints, 2 quarts, 6 quarts, 3 gallons.
    How much oil is left in the drum?
    _____ gallons.
    A. 0   B. 8   C. 45   D. 48

12. Suppose a certain chemical can be given out only in one kilogram containers. 2.2 pounds equals 1 kilogram.
    The GREATEST number of kilograms that can be obtained from 100 pounds of this chemical is MOST NEARLY
    A. 41   B. 43   C. 45   D. 47

13. A truckload of supplies weighing 1 1/2 tons is unloaded by 5 workers in 2 hours. Suppose that the work is equally divided among the workers.
    How many pounds of supplies can be unloaded by each worker per hour?
    _____ pounds per hour.
    A. 150   B. 300   C. 450   D. 600

14. A room is 40 yards long and 15 yards wide. One square foot of floor can support 100 pounds.
    What is the GREATEST weight that can be supported by the floor in that room?
    A. 600   B. 5,400   C. 60,000   D. 540,000

15. Suppose that an empty storage area can be safely loaded with 324,000 lbs. of stock items.
    How many boxes can be stored in this area if each box has in it one dozen cans that weigh 3 pounds each?
    A. 8,500   B. 9,000   C. 9,500   D. 10,000

16. 18 boxes of oranges with 1000 oranges in each box are in a storehouse.
    How many orders of 1,440 oranges each can be filled completely?
    A. 10   B. 11   C. 12   D. 13

17. Suppose that the following 3 deliveries of dry cereal are made each day: 30 cartons with 60 boxes in each carton, 25 cartons with 60 boxes in each carton, and 20 cartons with 100 boxes in each carton.
    If daily orders total 400 boxes, how many more boxes must be delivered in order to have enough boxes for a 14-day supply?

A. 50   B. 100   C. 200   D. 300

18. Suppose that 11 pints of distilled water are used each day in the hospital laboratories and that a pint costs 7 cents.
    What would a 30-day supply of distilled water cost?
    About

    A. $23   B. $24   C. $25   D. $27

18.____

19. If 2000 lbs. of salt costs $500, what does one pound cost?

    A. $.20   B. $.22   C. $.25   D. $.27

19.____

20. The price of floor wax is 15 cents a quart. On orders of over 100 gallons, however, 2.5% is subtracted from the price of every quart in the order.
    What is the cost of 200 gallons of floor wax?

    A. $115   B. $117   C. $119   D. $121

20.____

KEY (CORRECT ANSWERS)

1.	C	11.	D
2.	C	12.	C
3.	D	13.	B
4.	D	14.	D
5.	D	15.	B
6.	C	16.	C
7.	B	17.	D
8.	D	18.	A
9.	C	19.	C
10.	B	20.	B

TEST 4

DIRECTIONS: Each question or incomplete statement is followed by several suggested answers or completions. Select the one that BEST answers the question or completes the statement. *PRINT THE LETTER OF THE CORRECT ANSWER IN THE SPACE AT THE RIGHT.*

1. Employees who must lift and carry stock items should be careful to avoid injury. When an employee lifts or carries stock items, which of the following is the LEAST safe practice?

    A. Keep the legs straight and lift with the back muscles
    B. Keep the load as close to the body as possible
    C. Get a good grip on the object to be carried
    D. First determine if the item can be lifted and carried safely

    1._____

2. For warning and protection, the color red is usually used for

    A. indicating high temperature stockroom areas
    B. floor markings
    C. location of first aid supplies
    D. stop buttons, lights for barricades, and other dangerous locations

    2._____

3. Reporting rattles, squeaks, or other noises in equipment to your maintenance supervisor is

    A. *bad;* too much attention to squeaks like these keep important safety problems from being noticed
    B. *bad;* each person should oil and care for his own equipment
    C. *good;* these sounds may mean that the equipment should be fixed
    D. *good;* it shows the supervisor that you are a good worker

    3._____

4. If you often get cuts on your hands from handling different kinds of cartons and boxes, the BEST thing for you to do is

    A. keep from handling those kinds of cartons and boxes
    B. ask that better boxes and cartons be used
    C. toughen up your hands
    D. wear protective gloves

    4._____

5. A low, movable platform used for stacking material in a warehouse is called a *pallet*. When lifting and moving *pallets* with a forklift, how should a stockman place the forks?

    A. As wide apart as possible
    B. As close together as possible
    C. Close together and tilted forward
    D. Wide apart and tilted forward

    5._____

Questions 6-11.

DIRECTIONS: Questions 6 through 11 are to be answered ONLY on the information given in the following table.

RECORD OF INCOMING FREIGHT SHIPMENTS

Received	Purchase Order No.	Amount Prepaid	Amount To Be Collected	Shipper	No. of Items	Weight	Shippers' Catalog No.
1/7	9616	$15.10		Harding Grove Equip	14	170	28
1/12	3388		$ 2.00	People's Paper Inc.	10	50	091
1/12	8333		$106.19	Falls Office Supply	25	2500	701
2/2	7126		$ 9.00	Leigh Foods	175	4000	47
2/13	4964		$ 3.09	McBride Paper Co.	14	75	83
4/13	3380	$14.09		Central Hardware	14	1750	019
4/30	7261		$ 6.90	Northwestern Foods	121	2100	13
5/12	9166	$10.50		Harding Grove Equip.	15	50	36
5/17	6949		$ 4.19	Black's Paper Co.	40	65	743
5/31	6691		$ 20.00	Central Hardware	16	600	563
6/30	5388	$ 9.75		Harding Grove Equip.	15	15	420
6/30	8308		$ 22.50	Falls Office Supply	19	290	97
8/23	8553		$ 4.90	Tremont Paper Inc.	75	570	36
9/12	5338	$ 6.91		Northeast Hardware	51	901	071
10/15	6196	$12.00		Mobray Hardware	60	786	131

6. All items listed in the above table were delivered by 6.____

    A. U.S. mail   B. freight
    C. air express   D. ship

7. On what date was the LARGEST number of items received? 7.____

    A. 2/2   B. 2/13   C. 4/30   D. 5/17

8. If all items shipped by Falls Office Supply on 1/12 were of equal weight, how much did each item weigh? _____ pounds. 8.____

    A. 10   B. 25   C. 100   D. 250

9. If the names of the shippers were put in alphabetical order, which of the following should be put after McBride Paper Company? 9.____

   A. Northeast Hardware
   B. Leigh Foods
   C. Northwestern Foods
   D. Mobray Hardware

10. What is the purchase order number for the Harding Grove Equipment shipment that was received on 5/12? 10.____

   A. 9166
   B. 5388
   C. 9616
   D. 6691

11. All items that cost less than five dollars ($5.00) came from shippers of 11.____

   A. paper
   B. foods
   C. hardware
   D. office supplies

Questions 12-16.

DIRECTIONS: Questions 12 through 16 are to be answered SOLELY on the basis of the information contained in the following passage.

Floors in warehouses, storerooms, and shipping rooms must be strong enough to stay level under heavy loads. Unevenness of floors may cause boxes of materials to topple and fall. Safe floor load capacities and maximum heights to which boxes may be stacked should be posted conspicuously so all can notice it. Where material in boxes, containers, or cartons of the same weight is regularly stored, it is good practice to paint a horizontal line on the wall indicating the maximum height to which the material may be piled. A qualified expert should determine floor load capacity from the building plans, the age, and condition of the floor supports, the type of floor, and other related information.

Working aisles are those from which material is placed into and removed from storage. Working aisles are of two types: transportation aisles, running the length of the building, and cross aisles, running across the width of the building. Deciding on the number, width, and location of working aisles is important. While aisles are necessary and determine boundaries of storage areas, they reduce the space actually used for storage.

12. According to the passage above, how should safe floor load capacities be made known to employees? 12.____
    They should be

    A. given out to each employee
    B. given to supervisors only
    C. printed in large red letters
    D. posted so that they are easily seen

13. According to the passage above, floor load capacities should be determined by 13.____

    A. warehouse supervisors
    B. the fire department
    C. qualified experts
    D. machine operators

14. According to the above passage, transportation aisles 14.____

    A. run the length of the building
    B. run across the width of the building

C. are wider than cross aisles
D. are shorter than cross aisles

15. According to the passage above, working aisles tend to

    A. take away space that could be used for storage
    B. add to space that could be used for storage
    C. slow down incoming stock
    D. speed up outgoing stock

16. According to the passage above, unevenness of floors may cause

    A. overall warehouse deterioration
    B. piles of stock to fall
    C. materials to spoil
    D. many worker injuries

Questions 17-20.

DIRECTIONS: Questions 17 through 20 are to be answered SOLELY on the basis of the information contained in the following passage.

Planning for the unloading of incoming trucks is not easy since generally little or no advance notice of truck arrivals is received. The height of the floor of truck bodies and loading platforms sometimes are different; this makes necessary the use of special unloading methods. When available, hydraulic ramps compensate for the differences in platform and truck floor levels. When hydraulic ramps are not available, forklift equipment can sometimes be used, if the truck springs are strong enough to support such equipment. In a situation like this, the unloading operation does not differ much from unloading a railroad boxcar. In the cases where the forklift truck or a hydraulic pallet jack cannot be used inside the truck, a pallet dolly should be placed inside the truck, so that the empty pallet can be loaded close to the truck contents and rolled easily to the truck door and platform.

17. According to the passage above, unloading trucks is

    A. easy to plan since the time of arrival is usually known beforehand
    B. the same as loading a railroad boxcar
    C. hard to plan since trucks arrive without notice
    D. a very normal thing to do

18. According to the above passage, which materials handling equipment can make up for the difference in platform and truck floor levels?

    A. Hydraulic jacks   B. Hydraulic ramps
    C. Forklift trucks   D. Conveyors

19. According to the above passage, what materials handling equipment can be used when a truck cannot support the weight of forklift equipment?

    A. A pallet dolly   B. A hydraulic ramp
    C. Bridge plates   D. A warehouse tractor

20. Which is the BEST title for the above passage? 20._____
    A. Unloading Railroad Boxcars
    B. Unloading Motor Trucks
    C. Loading Rail Boxcars
    D. Loading Motor Trucks

KEY (CORRECT ANSWERS)

1.	B	11.	A
2.	D	12.	D
3.	C	13.	C
4.	D	14.	A
5.	A	15.	A
6.	B	16.	B
7.	A	17.	C
8.	C	18.	B
9.	D	19.	A
10.	A	20.	B

EXAMINATION SECTION
TEST 1

DIRECTIONS: Each question or incomplete statement is followed by several suggested answers or completions. Select the one that BEST answers the question or completes the statement. *PRINT THE LETTER OF THE CORRECT ANSWER IN THE SPACE AT THE RIGHT.*

1. The storage life of commodities in common dry storage is dependent in part upon the factors of temperature and humidity.
   In general, the MOST favorable combination of these two factors for storage purposes is _____ temperature and _____ humidity.

    A. high; low
    B. high; high
    C. low; high
    D. low; low

    1._____

2. Which one of the following is it MOST important to locate on the ground floor near the point of receipt?

    A. Difficult-to-handle and bulky items
    B. Items which are readily portable and marketable
    C. Lightweight items
    D. Low turnover items

    2._____

3. A basic reason for assigning commodity code numbers to purchased and stored items is to

    A. prevent pilferage
    B. increase the use of mechanized equipment
    C. facilitate ready reference in communications
    D. decrease flexibility of storage areas

    3._____

4. A straddle carry truck is MOST appropriately used in a warehouse or in a section of a warehouse handling

    A. automotive parts and tools
    B. paints and varnishes
    C. pipe and lumber
    D. stationery and paper

    4._____

5. In general, you would expect to find materials handling equipment to be equipped with solid rubber tires when used primarily

    A. for heavy-duty lifting, both indoors and outdoors
    B. for indoor operations
    C. in improved outdoor storage areas
    D. in unimproved outdoor storage areas

    5._____

6. Of the following, the MOST probable hazard in storing subsistence supplies, such as meats and cereal products, is

    A. breakage
    B. flammability
    C. spillage
    D. spoilage

    6._____

7. When operating a forklift truck, the one of the following which is LEAST hazardous is   7._____

   A. backing the truck slowly down a slight grade or ramp
   B. driving the truck with the forks highly elevated
   C. leaving the truck unattended, facing downhill, with the motor running
   D. trying to lift large loads with only one fork

8. Of the following, the one which is usually LEAST likely to be shown on properly maintained bin tags is the   8._____

   A. amount received   B. amount withdrawn
   C. anticipated yearly need   D. balance on hand

9. Special instructions for storage and release of dated items which are subject to spoilage are LEAST likely needed for   9._____

   A. batteries   B. brass couplings
   C. film   D. paint

10. Of the following rodent control measures, the one which is generally LEAST effective is   10._____

    A. eliminating sources of food and shelter for the rodents
    B. sealing holes around pipes and wires where rodents may enter the building
    C. setting traps for the rodents
    D. spraying all incoming stock with piperonyl butoxide to kill the rodents

11. Of the following, a well-managed storage operation is MOST likely to reduce the   11._____

    A. coordination between purchasing and stores operations
    B. idle time of operating personnel awaiting material
    C. turnover of stored materials
    D. utilization of mechanical aids

Questions 12-21.

DIRECTIONS: Questions 12 through 21 are to be answered SOLELY on the basis of the information given in the following table.

TABLE OF INFORMATION ABOUT GARDEN HOSE ON HAND

Commodity Index Number	Kind and Diameter of Hose (in inches)	Number of Feet Per Roll	Weight Per Roll lbs. ozs.		Cost Per Roll	Number of Rolls on Hand
SL 14171	Plastic, 3/4 in.	25	6	5	5.90	20
SL 14172	Plastic, 3/4 in.	50	12	5	9.90	50
SL 14271	Plastic, 5/8 in.	25	4	7	4.40	40
SL 14272	Plastic, 5/8 in.	50	8	10	7.40	50
SL 14273	Plastic, 5/8 in.	75	13	0	10.40	50
SL 14274	Plastic, 5/8 in.	100	17	0	13.40	100
SL 24171	Rubber, Reinforced, 3/4"	25	9	3	8.90	20
SL 24172	Rubber, Reinforced, 3/4"	50	18	0	14.90	10
SL 24271	Rubber, Reinforced, 5/8"	25	6	2	6.20	40
SL 24272	Rubber, Reinforced, 5/8"	50	12	2	10.90	40
SL 24273	Rubber, Reinforced, 5/8"	75	18	0	15.20	60
SL 24274	Rubber, Reinforced, 5/8"	100	24	0	19.90	100

12. The total number of 25 foot rolls of all types of garden hose currently on hand is

    A. 120   B. 180   C. 220   D. 400

12._____

13. The total weight of one roll each of SL 14172, SL 14273, SL 24271, and SL 24274 is _____ lbs. 7 ozs.

    A. 49   B. 51   C. 55   D. 61

13._____

14. The total weight of all of the 25 foot rolls of rubber, reinforced, 5/8 inch garden hose on hand is _____ lbs.

    A. 175   B. 240   C. 245   D. 485

14._____

15. An order for 10 rolls of SL 14271, 17 rolls of SL 14274, and 22 rolls of SL 24271 will MOST NEARLY weigh _____ lbs.

    A. 333   B. 423   C. 468   D. 472

15._____

16. The total cost of 12 rolls of 100 foot plastic, 5/8 inch garden hose is

    A. $124.80   B. $134.00   C. $160.80   D. $238.80

16._____

17. Assume that from the 40 rolls of SL 24272 and the 100 rolls of SL 24274 you ship one order of 10 rolls of SL 24272 and one order of 50 rolls of SL 24274.
The total cost of all of the SL 24272 and the SL 24274 garden hose still on hand, after filling these orders, is

   A. $479   B. $1,104   C. $1,322   D. $1,451

18. Assume that 15% of all the 100 foot rolls of plastic garden hose and rubber reinforced garden hose are found defective.
Then, the total cost of the defective hose is

   A. $199.00   B. $298.00   C. $333.00   D. $499.50

19. The stock on hand of which one of the following sizes and types of garden hose has the GREATEST total cost?
SL

   A. 14171   B. 14271   C. 24171   D. 24172

20. If 3/4 inch plastic garden hose is taken from the 50 foot rolls, then the cost of one foot of such hose is MOST NEARLY

   A. 20¢   B. 23¢   C. 26¢   D. 29¢

21. If it takes one worker one hour to inspect 20 rolls of garden hose for defects, the LEAST amount of time it will take two workers to inspect ALL the rolls of garden hose in stock is _____ hours _____ minutes.

   A. 14; 30   B. 15; 50   C. 24; 10   D. 29; 0

22. Assume that it takes two men forty hours to do a certain job. The time it will take five men to do the same job is _____ hours.

   A. 4   B. 8   C. 10   D. 16

23. Assume that a certain floor covering costs $5.00 per square yard. You order two pieces, one measuring 8 yards by 10 yards and the other measuring 9 yards by 6 yards. The total cost of the two pieces is

   A. $400   B. $570   C. $670   D. $970

24. Assume that you have received a delivery of sand, which took up the entire area of a trailer with interior dimensions of 40 feet by 7 feet and the sand was loaded to an average depth of 4 feet.
The amount of storage space, in cubic yards, required for this shipment of sand is MOST NEARLY _____ cubic yards.

   A. 42   B. 125   C. 374   D. 1,120

25. Assume that lubricating oil is delivered to your warehouse in 20 gallon drums. Requisitions for amounts less than 20 gallons are filled by drawing off the required amount of lubricating oil from one of the 20-gallon drums. After filling several requisitions for various amounts of lubricating oil, you find that you have on hand 18 full drums, 6 drums that are three-quarters full, 4 drums that are one-half full, and 8 drums that are one-quarter full. The total amount of lubricating oil that you have on hand is _____ gallons.

   A. 360   B. 530   C. 540   D. 600

KEY (CORRECT ANSWERS)

1. D
2. A
3. C
4. C
5. B

6. D
7. A
8. C
9. B
10. D

11. B
12. A
13. C
14. C
15. C

16. C
17. C
18. D
19. C
20. A

21. A
22. D
23. C
24. A
25. B

TEST 2

DIRECTIONS: Each question or incomplete statement is followed by several suggested answers or completions. Select the one that BEST answers the question or completes the statement. *PRINT THE LETTER OF THE CORRECT ANSWER IN THE SPACE AT THE RIGHT.*

Questions 1-13.

DIRECTIONS: Questions 1 through 13 are to be answered by choosing from the given classifications the one under which the item is MOST likely to be found in general stock catalogs.

1. *Chisels* may BEST be classified under

    A. food and condiments
    B. hand tools and accessories
    C. office machines and equipment
    D. stationery supplies

2. *Columnar pads* may BEST be classified under

    A. dry goods, textiles, and floor covering
    B. hospital and surgical supplies
    C. recreational supplies and equipment
    D. stationery and office supplies

3. *Gingham* may BEST be classified under

    A. clothing and textiles
    B. hand tools
    C. lighting apparatus
    D. paints and paint ingredients

4. *Trowels* may BEST be classified under

    A. dry goods and textiles
    B. hand tools and agricultural implements
    C. household supplies
    D. surgical supplies

5. *Collanders* may BEST be classified under

    A. building materials
    B. kitchen utensils
    C. motor vehicle parts
    D. plumbing supplies

6. *Litmus paper* may BEST be classified under

    A. laboratory supplies
    B. sewing supplies
    C. stationery and supplies
    D. textiles

7. *Pipettes* may BEST be classified under

    A. hardware
    B. hospital and laboratory supplies
    C. kitchen utensils and tableware
    D. plumbing fixtures and parts

8. *Carbon tetrachloride* may BEST be classified under   8.____

    A. brushes
    B. clothing and textiles
    C. drugs and chemicals
    D. toilet articles and accessories

9. *Curry powder* may BEST be classified under   9.____

    A. drugs and chemicals
    B. food and condiments
    C. paints and supplies
    D. surgical and dental supplies

10. *Planes* may BEST be classified under   10.____

    A. floor coverings   B. hand tools
    C. household utensils   D. plumbing fixtures

11. *Wing nuts* may BEST be classified under   11.____

    A. food and condiments   B. hardware supplies
    C. household utensils   D. sewing supplies

12. *Chambray* may BEST be classified under   12.____

    A. canned goods, food, and miscellaneous groceries
    B. brooms and brushes
    C. drugs and chemicals
    D. dry goods and textiles

13. *Shears* may BEST be classified under   13.____

    A. agricultural implements   B. clothing and textiles
    C. electrical parts   D. furniture

Questions 14-18.

DIRECTIONS: Questions 14 through 18 represent items appearing on requisitions received in a storehouse. Assume that you have a wide variety of each item named. Some important information is missing from each description. Without this missing information (NOT code number or account number), it would be difficult to select the appropriate item from the variety in stock. From the choices given, select the one that represents the missing additional information that would be MOST important and helpful in filling each requisition.

14. PAPER, copy, 100% sulphite sub 20, white   14.____

    A. bond or onionskin   B. ruled or unruled
    C. size of paper   D. two or three holes

15. NEEDLES, hard sewing, 20 to package   15.____

    A. cost   B. metallic composition
    C. purpose   D. size

16. BATTERY, dry cell, flashlight   16.____

    A. nature of covering   B. manufacturer's name
    C. shape of battery   D. size of battery

17. SCREWS, wood, gross in box, brass, 1/2", No. 2   17.____

    A. round or flat head
    B. size of bolt
    C. type of lumber for which used
    D. type of metal of which made

18. THREAD, SPOOL COTTON, hand sewing 6 cord, 500 yd., one dozen in box, #60   18.____

    A. color of thread
    B. size of needle's eye
    C. type of fabric to be sewn
    D. diameter of spool

19. If one dozen mops cost $14.00 and one gallon of floor wax costs $10.00, the total cost of five mops and three pints of floor wax is MOST NEARLY   19.____

    A. $9.60   B. $12.00   C. $13.30   D. $14.30

20. Assume that your warehouse issues paint in gallon cans and in quart cans. At the beginning of a certain week, you have 150 gallon cans and 100 quart cans of paint on hand. On Monday, you issue 10 gallon cans and 9 quart cans; on Tuesday, 9 gallon cans and 4 quart cans; on Wednesday, 4 gallon cans and 7 quart cans; on Thursday, 7 gallon cans and 11 quart cans; and on Friday, you issue 5 gallon cans and 5 quart cans.
    The total number of cans of paint on hand at the end of this week, assuming you have received no shipments of paint, is _____ gallon cans and _____ quart cans.   20.____

    A. 35; 36   B. 65; 64   C. 65; 86   D. 115; 64

21. A storage carton with dimensions of 1 foot 6 inches by 2 feet 4 inches by 4 feet has MOST NEARLY a volume of _____ cubic feet.   21.____

    A. 9.33   B. 10   C. 14   D. 15.36

22. Assume that you can purchase a gallon of turpentine for $1.70. A discount of 10% is given for purchases of 80 gallons or more.
    If you purchase 100 gallons of turpentine, the unit cost of one quart of turpentine is MOST NEARLY _____ cents.   22.____

    A. 38   B. 43   C. 77   D. 85

23. Assume that you have dispatched a truck at 9 A.M. to make a single delivery at a location which is 20 miles from your warehouse.
Assuming that the truck travels at an average speed of 15 miles per hour and that one-half is required to make the delivery, you should expect the truck to return to the warehouse at approximately

   A. 10:50 A.M.
   B. 11:40 A.M.
   C. 12:10 P.M.
   D. 12:40 P.M.

24. Assume that you are informed that on the next day at 9 A.M. you will receive six truckloads of goods. Two man-hours are required to unload each truckload of goods, and 6 man-hours are required to place each truckload of goods in storage.
If you plan to complete this task by 1:00 P.M., the minimum number of men that you should assign to this task is

   A. 4
   B. 8
   C. 12
   D. 16

25. Assume that you have in stock 15 one-gallon cans of rubber cement thinner. After filling an order for 50 bottles each containing 16 fluid ounces of rubber cement thinner, the amount of rubber cement thinner remaining in stock is

   A. none; you do not have enough stock to fill this order
   B. 1 gallon 1 quart
   C. 4 gallons 1 1/2 quarts
   D. 8 gallons 3 quarts

KEY (CORRECT ANSWERS)

1. B		11. B	
2. D		12. D	
3. A		13. A	
4. B		14. C	
5. B		15. D	
6. A		16. D	
7. B		17. A	
8. C		18. A	
9. B		19. A	
10. B		20. D	

21. C
22. A
23. C
24. C
25. D

EXAMINATION SECTION
TEST 1

DIRECTIONS: Each question or incomplete statement is followed by several suggested answers or completions. Select the one that BEST answers the question or completes the statement. *PRINT THE LETTER OF THE CORRECT ANSWER IN THE SPACE AT THE RIGHT.*

1. When picking items from a shelf at least 10 feet high, the one of the following that is BEST to use is a   1.____

    A. cart   B. table   C. stool   D. ladder

2. Cardboard boxes, wrapping paper, and cord are all very useful items in   2.____

    A. packaging   B. typing   C. cleaning   D. filing

Questions 3-6.

DIRECTIONS: Questions 3 through 6 are to be answered by picking the answer which is in the correct numerical order, from the lowest number to the highest number, in each question.

3. A. 44533, 44518, 44516, 44547
    B. 44516, 44518, 44533, 44547
    C. 44547, 44533, 44518, 44516
    D. 44518, 44516, 44547, 44533

4. A. 95587, 95593, 95601, 95620
    B. 95601, 95620, 95587, 95593
    C. 95593, 95587, 95601, 95620
    D. 95620, 95601, 95593, 95587

5. A. 232212, 232208, 232232, 232223
    B. 232208, 232223, 232212, 232232
    C. 232208, 232212, 232223, 232232
    D. 232223, 232232, 232208, 232212

6. A. 113419, 113521, 113462, 113588
    B. 113588, 113462, 113521, 113419
    C. 113521, 113588, 113419, 113462
    D. 113419, 113462, 113521, 113588

Questions 7-10.

DIRECTIONS: Questions 7 through 10 are to be answered on the basis of the information given below.

The most commonly used filing system and the one that is easiest to learn is alphabetical filing. This involves putting records in an A to Z order, according to the letters of the alphabet. The name of a person is filed by using the following order: first, the surname or last name; second, the first name; third, the middle name or middle initial. For example, *Henry C. Young* is filed under *Y* and thereafter under *Young, Henry C.* The name of a company is filed in the same way. For example, *Long Cabinet Co.* is filed under L, while *John T. Long Cabinet Co.* is filed under *L* and thereafter under *Long, John T. Cabinet Co.*

7. The one of the following which lists the names of persons in the CORRECT alphabetical order is

    A. Mary Carrie, Helen Carrol, James Carson, John Carter
    B. James Carson, Mary Carrie, John Carter, Helen Carrol
    C. Helen Carrol, James Carson, John Carter, Mary Carrie
    D. John Carter, Helen Carrol, Mary Carrie, James Carson

8. The one of the following which lists the names of persons in the CORRECT alphabetical order is

    A. Jones, John C.; Jones, John A.; Jones, John P.; Jones, John K.
    B. Jones, John P.; Jones, John K.; Jones, John C.; Jones, John A.
    C. Jones, John A.; Jones, John C.; Jones, John K.; Jones, John P.
    D. Jones, John K.; Jones, John C.; Jones, John A.; Jones, John P.

9. The one of the following which lists the names of the companies in the CORRECT alphabetical order is

    A. Blane Co., Blake Co., Block Co., Blear Co.
    B. Blake Co., Blane Co., Blear Co., Block Co.
    C. Block Co., Blear Co., Blane Co., Blake Co.
    D. Blear Co., Blake Co., Blane Co., Block Co.

10. You are to return to the file an index card on *Barry C. Wayne Materials and Supplies Co.* Of the following, the CORRECT alphabetical group that you should return the index card to is

    A. A to G
    B. H to M
    C. N to S
    D. T to Z

11. If 75 crates of food were ordered and 100 crates were delivered, then the shipment is larger than the number ordered by _____ crates.

    A. 10   B. 15   C. 25   D. 35

12. If 200 boxes of merchandise were ordered and 100 boxes are delivered, then the shipment is short by _____ boxes.

    A. 50   B. 100   C. 150   D. 175

13. You should be careful when storing food items which give off odors.
    Of the following, the food item which is MOST likely to give off a strong odor is

    A. baking powder   B. butter
    C. garlic   D. starch

14. Of the following, the one which is NOT an example of equipment generally used in preventing or fighting fires is a(n) 14.____

    A. extinguisher
    B. smoke alarm
    C. overhead sprinkler
    D. air pump

Questions 15-17.

DIRECTIONS: Questions 15 through 17 are to be answered on the basis of the information given below.

You are instructed to pack several items in a large shipping box. You are to pack the items as follows: items weighing 9 to 12 pounds are to be packed at the bottom of the box; items weighing 5 to 8 pounds are to be packed in the middle of the box; items weighing up to 4 pounds are to be packed at the top of the box. Any item weighing more than 12 pounds is to be packed in a separate box.

15. Based on the above instructions, an item weighing 3 pounds should be packed _____ box. 15.____

    A. at the bottom of the
    B. in the middle of the
    C. at the top of the
    D. in a separate

16. Based on the above instructions, an item weighing 10 pounds should be packed _____ box. 16.____

    A. at the bottom of the
    B. in the middle of the
    C. at the top of the
    D. in a separate

17. Based on the above instructions, an item weighing 13 pounds should be packed _____ box. 17.____

    A. at the bottom of the
    B. in the middle of the
    C. at the top of the
    D. in a separate

18. The color that BEST indicates *DANGER* and which generally appears on emergency stop buttons of electrical equipment is 18.____

    A. green   B. black   C. red   D. brown

19. Of the following, the material that would be MOST easily damaged if it becomes wet is 19.____

    A. plastic   B. rubber   C. glass   D. wood

20. The length of time for which whole milk can be stored under refrigeration without becoming spoiled is MOST NEARLY one 20.____

    A. day   B. week   C. month   D. year

21. You are told by your supervisor to unpack and check a box of 100 glass jars. While unwrapping the glass jars, you find that two of them are broken. 21.____
    The BEST action for you to take FIRST is to

    A. rewrap the broken glass jars and put them back in the box
    B. get rid of the broken glass jars
    C. report the breakage to your supervisor
    D. try to repair the broken glass jars

22. For safety reasons, the BEST kind of shoes to wear while working in a warehouse are

    A. medium-heeled, slip-on loafers with smooth leather soles
    B. low-heeled, slip-on moccasins
    C. high-heeled, dressy lace-up shoes
    D. low-heeled, lace-up shoes with non-skid soles

23. Your supervisor tells you to put an item back in its proper storage place. However, you do not know where the item is to be put back.
    Of the following, the BEST action for you to take is to

    A. put the item somewhere and forget about it
    B. ask your supervisor exactly where the item should be put back
    C. put the item in a separate box on the nearest shelf
    D. give the item to someone else to put back

24. You are to load a hand truck with cartons weighing a total of 200 pounds.
    If each carton weighs 20 pounds, then the TOTAL number of cartons to be loaded is

    A. 8   B. 9   C. 10   D. 11

25. You are to unpack twelve cartons of paper and place the paper on a storage shelf.
    If each carton has eight packs of paper, then the number of packs of paper that you will place on the shelf is

    A. 72   B. 84   C. 96   D. 108

26. If floor wax costs $2.90 a gallon, then the TOTAL cost of a carton in which there are six gallons of wax is

    A. $17.40   B. $19.00   C. $21.40   D. $29.00

27. You know that a storage shelf unit can safely hold items up to a total weight of 300 pounds.
    If there are already 8 boxes of canned food on the shelves of the unit, all exactly the same, and each box weighs 25 pounds, then the number of the same boxes of canned food that you can safely add to those on the shelves is

    A. 4   B. 5   C. 6   D. 7

28. When lifting a heavy box from the floor, you should place the box as _____ you as possible.

    A. much to the left of   B. much to the right of
    C. far away from   D. close to

29. You are asked by your supervisor to store some packages on a high shelf, which you will need a ladder to reach. When you find the ladder in your work area, you notice that it is in very bad condition. Some of the steps are very loose and need to be fixed.
    Of the following, the BEST action for you to take is to

    A. ask a co-worker to hold the ladder while you are using it
    B. tell your supervisor about the ladder and ask where another one can be found
    C. put the ladder aside and try to climb the shelves to store the packages
    D. take a chance and use the ladder to store the packages

Questions 30-35.

DIRECTIONS: Questions 30 through 35 are to be answered by choosing for your answer to each question the classification that BEST fits the stock item.

30. *Eggs* may BEST be classified under

    A. food and dairy
    B. metals
    C. chemicals
    D. paints and brushes

31. *Aspirin* may BEST be classified under

    A. kitchenware
    B. drugs
    C. plumbing supplies
    D. electrical supplies

32. *Oral thermometers* may BEST be classified under

    A. fire extinguishers
    B. cleaning equipment
    C. lumber supplies
    D. hospital supplies

33. *Paper clips* may BEST be classified under

    A. lighting equipment
    B. oils and greases
    C. office supplies
    D. gardening materials

34. *Hammer* may BEST be classified under

    A. liquids
    B. food products
    C. tools
    D. glass products

35. *Carburetors* may BEST be classified under _____ equipment.

    A. welding
    B. automotive
    C. laboratory
    D. building

KEY (CORRECT ANSWERS)

1.	D	16.	A
2.	A	17.	D
3.	B	18.	C
4.	A	19.	D
5.	C	20.	B
6.	D	21.	C
7.	A	22.	D
8.	C	23.	B
9.	B	24.	C
10.	D	25.	C
11.	C	26.	A
12.	B	27.	A
13.	C	28.	D
14.	D	29.	B
15.	C	30.	A

31. B
32. D
33. C
34. C
35. B

TEST 2

DIRECTIONS: Each question or incomplete statement is followed by several suggested answers or completions. Select the one that BEST answers the question or completes the statement. *PRINT THE LETTER OF THE CORRECT ANSWER IN THE SPACE AT THE RIGHT.*

1. Your supervisor has told you that food items, as they are received, should be dated on the outside of each package by the receiver. You are also told that you should always take the oldest food items first when you pick items from stock.
Based on the above information, the BEST way to find the *oldest* stock is to

    A. check the date on each package
    B. open each package and check the items inside
    C. find out from the receiver
    D. ask your supervisor

1.____

2. Your supervisor assigns you to unload a truck containing 10 cartons of medical supplies. While unloading the truck, you notice that one carton of medical supplies is open. All of the other cartons are sealed.
Of the following, the BEST action for you to take is to

    A. seal the carton neatly and continue to unload the truck
    B. report this matter to your supervisor
    C. hide the open carton and say nothing about the matter
    D. leave the carton open and store it with the other cartons

2.____

3. You are told to move an empty 55-gallon drum, which is on its side, a short distance. Of the following, the BEST way to move the drum while keeping control is for you to use your

    A. hands   B. feet   C. shoulder   D. back

3.____

4. You are told to unpack two boxes which, according to the purchase order and the invoice, are supposed to contain four gallons of paint each. However, you find that there are six gallons of paint in each box.
Of the following, the MOST reasonable course of action for you to take is to

    A. put all the paint in storage until someone finds out about the error
    B. store only the paint which has been ordered and keep the extra paint for yourself
    C. tell your supervisor about the extra gallons of paint that you found in each box
    D. give the extra gallons of paint to those whom you know can use them

4.____

5. When receiving a delivery of goods, it will usually be necessary for you to do the following tasks:
    I. Stock the goods on the storage shelf
    II. Unload the goods from the truck
    III. Take the goods to the storage area

    Which one of the following shows the CORRECT order in which you should do the tasks listed above?

    A. I, II, and III   B. II, III, and I
    C. III, II, and I   D. II, I, and III

5.____

63

6. You are on the top of a 6-foot ladder and are about to put a 30-pound box on a high shelf when the telephone rings. There is no one else around to answer it.
Of the following, the BEST course of action for you to take is to _____ answer the telephone.

    A. come down off the ladder with the box and
    B. put the box on the shelf and then come down from the ladder to
    C. let the box fall to the floor and then come down from the ladder to
    D. come down off the ladder with the box and see if you can find someone else to

Questions 7-9.

DIRECTIONS: Questions 7 through 9 are to be answered on the basis of the following charts and information.

AREA 1

Section A	Section B
stationery	electrical supplies
office supplies	lighting equipment
kitchenware	dry goods

AREA 2

Section A	Section B
drugs	tools
chemicals	laboratory equipment
cleaning supplies	hospital supplies

The above charts represent a storage room which is separated into two areas, Area 1 and Area 2, and separated within each area into two sections, Section A and Section B. Each section stores the items shown on the charts.

7. According to the above charts, you should find *laboratory equipment* in Area _____, Section _____.

    A. 1; A   B. 1; B   C. 2; A   D. 2; B

8. According to the above charts, all of the following items are in Area 1, Section A EXCEPT

    A. dry goods   B. stationery
    C. kitchenware   D. office supplies

9. According to the above charts, you should store light bulbs in Area _____, Section _____.

    A. 1; A   B. 1; B   C. 2; A   D. 2; B

Questions 10-12.

DIRECTIONS: Questions 10 through 12 are to be answered on the basis of the information given in the stock listing below.

STOCK LISTING OF BOLTS, NUTS, SCREWS, WASHERS, ETC.

Item No.	Commodity Code	Description
1	43-A00059	Anchor Expansion Mach Screw Type 6/32 inch
2	43-A00061	Anchor Expansion Mach Screw Type 8/32 inch
3	43-B06028	Bolt Carriage Oval HD Hex Nut 3/16 x 1 inch
4	43-B06029	Bolt Carriage Oval HD Hex Nut 3/16 x $1\frac{1}{2}$ inch
5	43-N06033	Nut Mach Screw Brass Hex 4/40 inch
6	43-N04725	Nut Mach Screw Brass Hex 6/40 inch
7	43-S08963	Screw Mach Brass Rnd HD 6/32 x 1 inch
8	43-S08975	Screw Mach Brass Rnd HD 6/32 x 2 inch
9	43-W00700	Washer Brass Round 1 lb Pkg No. 4
10	43-W03024	Washer Brass Round 1 lb Pkg No. 6

10. The type of item which is described as *1 lb Pkg* is a

    A. bolt   B. nut   C. screw   D. washer

11. The Commodity Code which appears in the next row below Commodity Code 43-B06029 is

    A. 43-A00061   B. 43-B06028
    C. 43-N06033   D. 43-N04725

12. The one of the following which does NOT have the complete information taken from the *Description* column of the item is

    A. Anchor Expansion Mach Screw Type 8/32 inch

    B. Bolt Carriage Oval Nut 3/16 x $1\frac{1}{2}$ inch

    C. Nut Mach Screw Brass Hex 6/40 inch
    D. Screw Mach Brass Rnd HD 6/32 x 2 inch

Questions 13-17.

DIRECTIONS: Questions 13 through 17 are to be answered on the basis of the following diagram and information.

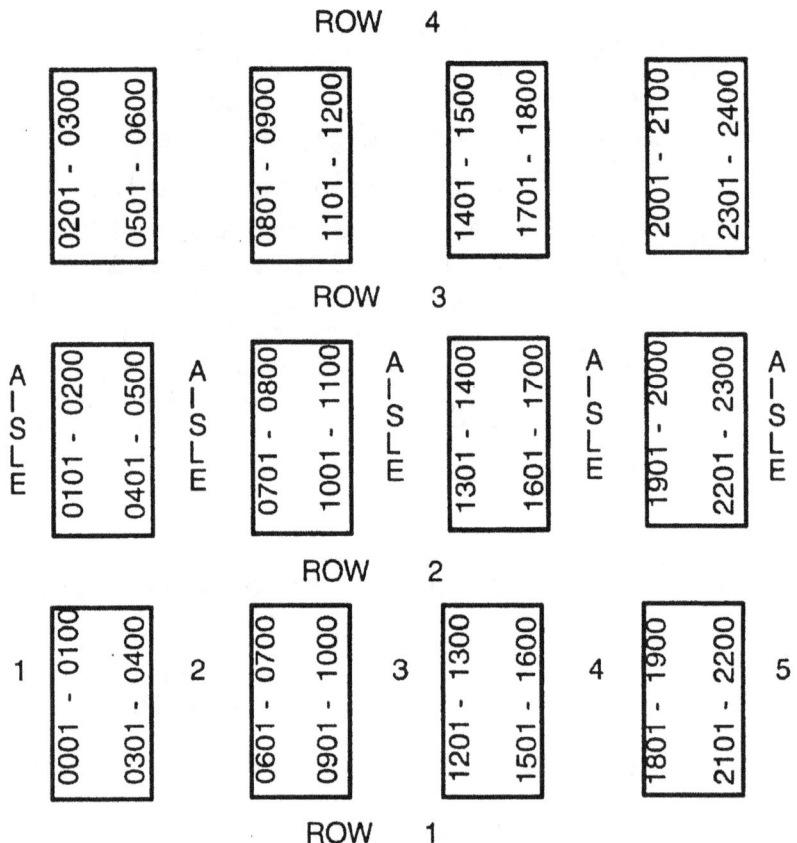

The above diagram represents a warehouse which has 4 Rows and 5 Aisles. Items are stored in this warehouse according to their item numbers which are shown in groups along the sides of the aisles. To find an item, you must go to the aisle and rows between which the item is located. For example, to find item number 0078, you must go to Aisle 1, between Rows 1 and 2, because item number 0078 is in group 0001 - 0100.

13. To find item number 1657, you should go to Aisle _____, between Rows _____. 13.____

   A. 1; 1 and 2
   B. 2; 2 and 3
   C. 4; 2 and 3
   D. 5; 1 and 2

14. To find item number 0723, you should go to Aisle _____, between Rows _____. 14.____

   A. 2; 1 and 2
   B. 2; 2 and 3
   C. 4; 2 and 3
   D. 4; 3 and 4

15. To find item number 1445, you should go to Aisle _____ , between Rows _____ .   15.____

    A. 1; 3 and 4   B. 2; 3 and 4
    C. 3; 3 and 4   D. 4; 3 and 4

16. To find item number 1201, you should go to Aisle _____ , between Rows _____ .   16.____

    A. 3; 1 and 2   B. 2; 3 and 4
    C. 5; 1 and 2   D. 4; 3 and 4

17. To find item number 2325, you should go to Aisle _____ , between Rows _____ .   17.____

    A. 2; 1 and 2   B. 3; 3 and 4
    C. 4; 1 and 2   D. 5; 3 and 4

Questions 18-20.

DIRECTIONS: Questions 18 through 20 are to be answered on the basis of the information given in the chart shown below.

Item	Weight
Metal file box	5 pounds
Large desk stapler	2 pounds
Large tape dispenser	1.5 pounds
Hardcover dictionary	3 pounds

18. Based on the figures shown in the chart above, the TOTAL weight of 5 metal file boxes, 3 hardcover dictionaries, and a large tape dispenser is _____ pounds.   18.____

    A. 33.5   B. 34.5   C. 35.5   D. 36.5

19. Of the following, which group of items would weigh a TOTAL of 25 pounds or less?   19.____

    A. 6 metal file boxes and 1 hardcover dictionary
    B. 10 large desk staplers and 1 hardcover dictionary
    C. 8 hardcover dictionaries and 2 large tape dispensers
    D. 10 large tape dispensers and 3 metal file boxes

20. Assume that 5 large desk staplers, 6 metal file boxes, 10 hardcover dictionaries, and 3 large tape dispensers are placed in a shipping container with a weight limit of 100 pounds.
When you add up the total weight of the items, the number of pounds under the weight limit would be _____ pounds.   20.____

    A. 23.5   B. 24.5   C. 25.5   D. 26.5

Questions 21-25.

DIRECTIONS: Questions 21 through 25 are to be answered on the basis of the information given in the stock listing below.

LISTING OF ENVELOPES IN STOCK

Item No.	Description	Unit of Issue	Amount
1	Envelope Commercial White 3 5/8" x $6\frac{1}{2}$"	1000 per carton	14 cartons
2	Envelope Commercial White $4\frac{1}{2}$" x $9\frac{1}{2}$"	2500 per carton	7 cartons
3	Envelope Open End Metal Clasp 7" x 10"	1000 per carton	16 cartons
4	Envelope Open End Metal Clasp $8\frac{1}{2}$" x $11\frac{1}{2}$"	1000 per carton	15 cartons
5	Envelope Open End Metal Clasp $9\frac{1}{2}$" x $12\frac{1}{2}$"	500 per carton	28 cartons
6	Envelope Open End Metal Clasp $11\frac{1}{2}$" x $4\frac{1}{2}$"	500 per carton	24 cartons

21. The TOTAL number of cartons of envelopes in stock is

    A. 87   B. 84   C. 100   D. 104

21.____

22. The envelopes which all have a unit of issue of 1000 per carton are found in Item Nos.

    A. 1, 2, and 3   B. 1, 3, and 4
    C. 2, 4, and 5   D. 3, 4, and 6

22.____

23. The item for which there is the GREATEST number of envelopes in stock is Item No.

    A. 2   B. 3   C. 4   D. 5

23.____

24. The TOTAL number of envelopes in stock for all of the items listed above is

    A. 74,000   B. 81,000   C. 88,500   D. 104,500

24.____

25. You receive an order for the following items: Item No. 1, 2000 envelopes; Item No. 2, 5000 envelopes; Item No. 4, 2000 envelopes; Item No. 6, 1000 envelopes.
The TOTAL number of cartons that you will have to pick from stock in filling the order is

    A. 6   B. 7   C. 8   D. 9

25.____

Questions 26-33.

DIRECTIONS: Questions 26 through 33 are to be answered on the basis of the following blank ORDER FOR SUPPLIES form and information.

ORDER FOR SUPPLIES

Agency 1	Date 2	Agency Order No. 3
Expected Date of Delivery 4	Unit 5	Agency Address 6
Item No 7	Description of Item 8	No. of Items Ordered 9
Line 1		
Line 2		
Line 3		
Line 4		
Line 5		
Items Picked By 10 Name____ Date____	Items Packed By 11 Name____ Date____	Items Received By 12 Name____ Date____

On September 3, Agency A, located at 220 Reade Street in Manhattan, orders the following items:

Item No.	Description of Item	No. of Items Ordered
65	Large roll of scotch tape	50
21	Desk calendar refill	73
20	Desk blotter	40
18	12-inch wooden ruler	36
17	Desk stapler	15

The agency order number is 000177A. The expected date of delivery is November 5. The items are ordered by the Accounting Unit of Agency A. The items are picked by J. Hines on October 20. The items are packed by L. Warren on October 21. The items are received by G. Westerly on November 3.

26. The date which should appear in Box 10 on the form is

    A. October 20   B. October 21
    C. November 3   D. November 5

27. The agency order number which should appear in Box 3 is

    A. 00117A   B. 00017A   C. 00177A   D. 000177A

28. The date of November 5 should appear in Box

    A. 2   B. 4   C. 11   D. 12

29. If the item numbers are written in Box 7 on Lines 1 through 5, from the lowest to the highest number, then the Item No. that should appear on Line 3 is

    A. 17   B. 20   C. 21   D. 65

30. The person whose name should appear in Box 11 is

    A. L. Warren   B. J. Hines
    C. G. Westerly   D. A. Haynes

31. For which one of the following is the number of items ordered the SMALLEST?

    A. Large roll of scotch tape
    B. Desk calendar refill
    C. 12-inch wooden ruler
    D. Desk stapler

32. The one of the following which is the CORRECT street address that should appear in Box 6 is _____ Street.

    A. 220 Reade
    B. 202 Read
    C. 220 Reed
    D. 202 Rade

33. The time from the date the items were ordered to the date the items were received was MOST NEARLY

    A. 2 days   B. 6 weeks   C. 2 months   D. 6 months

34. A storeroom has 12 rows of boxes with 8 boxes in each row. Each box contains 14 cartons of juice.
    The TOTAL number of cartons of juice in the storeroom is

    A. 112   B. 168   C. 672   D. 1344

35. There is shelf space available that measures 60 inches wide, 20 inches deep, and 20 inches high.
    If you have a carton that measures 18 inches wide, 18 inches deep, and 18 inches high, then the number of cartons you can put on the shelf is MOST NEARLY

    A. 2   B. 3   C. 4   D. 5

KEY (CORRECT ANSWERS)

1. A	11. C	21. D	31. D
2. B	12. B	22. B	32. A
3. A	13. C	23. A	33. C
4. C	14. B	24. C	34. D
5. B	15. C	25. C	35. B
6. B	16. A	26. A	
7. D	17. D	27. D	
8. A	18. C	28. B	
9. B	19. B	29. B	
10. D	20. C	30. A	

ARITHMETICAL REASONING
EXAMINATION SECTION
TEST 1

DIRECTIONS: Each question or incomplete statement is followed by several suggested answers or completions. Select the one that BEST answers the question or completes the statement. *PRINT THE LETTER OF THE CORRECT ANSWER IN THE SPACE AT THE RIGHT.*

1. Assume that it takes approximately 1 1/2 minutes to unload a dozen identical items from a delivery truck.
   At this speed, the amount of time it should take to unload a shipment of 876 items is, MOST NEARLY, _____ minutes.
   A. 90   B. 100   C. 110   D. 120

   1.____

2. Assume that a shop clerk has received a bill of $108 for a delivery of clamps which cost $4.32 per dozen.
   How many clamps should there be in this delivery?
   A. 25   B. 36   C. 300   D. 360

   2.____

3. Employee A has not used any leave time and has accumulated a total of 45 leave-days.
   How many months did it take employee A to have accumulated 45 leave-days if the accrual rate is 1 2/3 days per months?
   A. 25   B. 27   C. 29   D. 31

   3.____

4. A shop clerk is notified that only 75 bolts can be supplied by Vendor A.
   If this represents 12.5% of the total requisition, then how many bolts were originally ordered?
   A. 125   B. 600   C. 700   D. 900

   4.____

5. An enclosed square-shaped storage area with sides of 16 feet each has a safe-load capacity of 250 pounds per square foot.
   The MAXIMUM evenly distributed weight that can be stored in this area is _____ lbs.
   A. 1,056   B. 4,000   C. 64,000   D. 102,400

   5.____

6. A clerical employee completed 70 progress reports the first week, 87 the second week, and 80 the third week.
   Assuming a 4-week month, how many progress reports must the clerk complete in the fourth week in order to attain an average of 85 progress reports per week for the month?
   A. 93   B. 103   C. 113   D. 133

   6.____

7. On the first of the month, Shop X received a delivery of 150 gallons of lubricating oil. During the month, the following amounts of oil were used on lubricating work each week: 30 quarts, 36 quarts, 20 quarts, and 48 quarts.
The amount of lubricating oil remaining at the end of the month was _____ gallons.
    A. 4
    B. 33.5
    C. 41.5
    D. 116.5

8. For working a 35-hour week, Employee A earns a gross amount of $160.30. For each hour that Employee A works over 40 hours a week, he is entitled to 1 1/2 times his hourly wage rate.
If Employee A worked 9 hours on Monday, 8 hours on Tuesday, 9 hours 30 minutes on Wednesday, 9 hours 15 minutes on Thursday, and 9 hours 15 minutes on Friday, what should his gross salary be for that week?
    A. $206.10
    B. $210.68
    C. $217.55
    D. $229.00

9. An enclosed cube-shaped storage bay has dimensions of 12 feet by 12 feet by 12 feet. Standard procedure requires that there be at least 1 foot of space between the walls, the ceiling and the stored items.
What is the MAXIMUM number of cube-shaped boxes with length, width, and height of 1 foot each that can be stored on 1-foot high pallets in this bay?
    A. 1,000
    B. 1,331
    C. 1,452
    D. 1,728

10. Assume that two ceilings are to be painted. One ceiling measures 30 feet by 15 feet and the second 45 feet by 60 feet.
If one quart of paint will cover 60 square feet of ceiling, approximately how much paint will be required to paint the two ceilings?
    A. 6 gallons
    B. 10 gallons
    C. 13 gallons
    D. 18 gallons

KEY (CORRECT ANSWERS)

1.	C	6.	B
2.	C	7.	D
3.	B	8.	C
4.	B	9.	A
5.	C	10.	C

SOLUTIONS TO PROBLEMS

1. $876 \div 12 = 73$. Then, $(73)(1\ 1/2) = 109.5 \approx 110$ minutes.

2. $\$108 \div \$4.32 = 25$. Then, $(25)(12) = 300$ clamps.

3. $45 \div 1\ 1/2 = 27$ months

4. $75 \div .125 = 600$ bolts

5. $(16)(16)(250) == 64,000$ pounds

6. $(85)(4) = 340$. Then, $340 - 70 - 87 - 80 = 103$ progress reports.

7. Changing every calculation to gallons, the amount of oil remaining is $150 - 7.5 - 9 - 5 - 12 = 116.5$.

8. $9 + 8 + 9.5 + 9.25 + 9.25 = 45$ hours. His gross pay will be $(\$4.58)(40) + (\$6.87)(5) = \$217.55$. (Note: To get his regular hourly wages, divide $\$160.30$ by 35.)

9. $12 - 1 - 1 = 10$. Maximum number of boxes is $(10)^3 = 1000$.

10. First ceiling contains $(30)(15) = 450$ sq.ft., whereas the second ceiling contains $(45)(60) = 2700$ sq.ft. The total sq.ft. = 3150. Now, $3150 \div 60 = 52.5$ quarts of paint = 13.125 or 13 gallons.

TEST 2

DIRECTIONS: Each question or incomplete statement is followed by several suggested answers or completions. Select the one that BEST answers the question or completes the statement. *PRINT THE LETTER OF THE CORRECT ANSWER IN THE SPACE AT THE RIGHT.*

1. A piping sketch is drawn to a scale of 1/8" = 1 foot.
   A vertical steam line measuring 3/4" on the sketch would have an actual length of _____ feet.
      A. 16   B. 22   C. 24   D. 28

   1._____

2. Three lengths of pipe 1'10", 3'2 1/2", and 5'7 1/2", respectively, are to be cut from a pipe 14'0" long.
   Allowing 1/8" for each pipe cut, the length of pipe remaining is
      A. 3'1 1/8"   B. 3'2 1/2"   C. 3'3 1/2"   D. 3'3 5/8"

   2._____

3. Assume that a steamfitter's helper earns $11.16 an hour and that he works 250 seven-hour days a year.
   His gross yearly salary will be
      A. 19,430   B. $19,530   C. $19,650   D. $19,780

   3._____

4. A pipe having an inside diameter of 3.48 inches and a wall thickness of .18 inches, will have an outside diameter of _____ inches.
      A. 3.84   B. 3.64   C. 3.57   D. 3.51

   4._____

5. A rectangular steel bar having a volume of 30 cubic inches, a width of 2 inches, and a height of 3 inches will have a length of _____ inches.
      A. 12   B. 10   C. 8   D. 5

   5._____

6. A pipe weighs 20.4 pounds per foot of length.
   The total weight of eight pieces of this pipe with each piece 20 feet in length is MOST NEARLY _____ pounds.
      A. 460   B. 1680   C. 2420   D. 3260

   6._____

7. In last year's budget, $7,500 was spent for office supplies. Of this amount, 60% was spent for paper supplies.
   If the price of paper has risen 20% over last year's price, then the amount that will be spent this year on paper supplies, assuming the same quantity will be purchased, will be
      A. $3,600   B. $5,200   C. $5,400   D. $6,000

   7._____

8. If it takes 4 painters 54 days to do a certain paint job, then the time it should take 5 painters working at the same speed to do the same job is MOST NEARLY _____ days.
      A. 3 1/2   B. 4   C. 4 1/2   D. 5

   8._____

2 (#2)

9. A foreman assigns a gang foreman to supervise a job which must be completed at the end of 7 working days. The gang foreman has 8 maintainers in his gang. At the end of 3 working days, although the work has been efficiently done, the job is only one-third completed.
   In order to complete the job on time, without overtime, the gang foreman should request that he be given _____ more maintainers.
   A. 3 B. 4 C. 5 D. 6

10. One shipment of 70 shovels costs $140. A second shipment of 130 shovels costs $208.00.
    The average cost per shovel for both shipments is MOST NEARLY
    A. $1.60 B. $1.75 C. $2.00 D. $2.50

KEY (CORRECT ANSWERS)

1.	D	6.	D
2.	D	7.	C
3.	B	8.	C
4.	A	9.	B
5.	D	10.	B

3 (#2)

SOLUTIONS TO PROBLEMS

1. 3 1/2 ÷ 1/8 = 28 feet.

2. 14' − 1'10" − 3' 1/2" − 5'7 1/2" − 1/8" − 1/8" − 1/8" = 3'3 5/8"

3. (250(7) = 1750 hours. Then, ($11.16)(1750) = $19,530

4. Outside diameter = 3.48 + .18 + .18 = 3.84 inches

5. Length is 30 ÷ 2 ÷ 3 = 5 inches

6. (20)(8) = 160 feet. Then, (160)(20.4) = 3264 ≈ 3260 pounds

7. ($7,500)(.60) = $4,500. Then, ($4,500)(1.20) = $5,400

8. Let x = required days. Since this is an inverse ratio, 4/5 = x/5 1/2. Then, 5x = 22.
   Solving, x = 4.4 ≈ 4 1/2

9. (8)(3) = 24 man-days were needed to complete 1/3 of the job.
   Since 2/3 of the job remains, the foreman will need 48 man-days for the remaining 4 days.
   This requires 12 men. Since he has 8 currently, he will need 4 more workers.

10. Average cost per shovel is ($140 + $208) ÷ (70+130) = $1.74, which is closest to $1.75.

TEST 3

DIRECTIONS: Each question or incomplete statement is followed by several suggested answers or completions. Select the one that BEST answers the question or completes the statement. *PRINT THE LETTER OF THE CORRECT ANSWER IN THE SPACE AT THE RIGHT.*

1. Assume that your warehouse received a shipment of 600 articles. A sample of 60 articles was inspected. Of this sample, one article was wholly defective and four articles were partly defective.
   On the basis of this sampling, you would expect the total number of defective articles in this shipment to be
   A. 5   B. 10   C. 40   D. 50

   1.____

2. Assume that you have been instructed to order mineral spirits as soon as the supply-on-hand falls to the level required for sixty days of issue.
   If the total amount of mineral spirits on hand is 960 gallons and you issue an average of 8 gallons of mineral spirits per day, and your warehouse works a five-day week, you will be required to order mineral spirits in _____ working days.
   A. 50   B. 60   C. 70   D. 80

   2.____

3. Assume that you work in a one-story warehouse where the total available floor space measures 175 feet by 140 feet. Of this floor space, one area measuring 35 feet by 75 feet is used for storing materials handling equipment, another area is measuring 10 feet by 21 feet is used for office space, and the remaining floor space is available for storage.
   The amount of floor space available for storage in this one-story warehouse is _____ square feet.
   A. 21,665   B. 21,875   C. 24,290   D. $24,500

   3.____

4. Assume that linoleum tiles measuring 9 inches by 9 inches are packed ten to a box and each box costs $3.50.
   The cost of buying enough linoleum tiles to cover an area measuring 15 feet by 21 feet is
   A. $98.00   B. $110.25   C. $196.00   D. $220.50

   4.____

5. The number of boxes measuring 3 inches by 3 inches by 3 inches that will fit into a carton measuring 2 feet by 4 feet is
   A. 2,048   B. 2,645   C. 7,936   D. 23,808

   5.____

6. The stock inventory card for paint, white, flat, one-gallon, has the following entries:

Date	Received	Shipped	Balance
April 12	-	25	75
April 13	50	75	
April 14	-	10	
April 15	25		
April 16			

   6.____

2 (#3)

The balance on hand at the close of business on April 15 should be
A. 40   B. 45   C. 55   D. 65

7. The cost of one dozen pieces of screening, each measuring 4 feet 6 inches at $.10 per square foot is
A. $22.50   B. $25.00   C. $27.00   D. $27.60

8. Assume that it takes an average of ten man-hours to stack four tons of a particular item.
In order to stack 80 tons, the number of men required to complete the job in twenty hours is
A. 10   B. 20   C. 30   D. 40

9. Assume that you are required to relocate 5,000 reams of unboxed paper using only manual labor. The average time required for one laborer to pick 12 reams, carry them to the new location, and store them properly is ten minutes.
In order to complete this relocation task within one working day of seven hours, the MINIMUM number of laborers you should assign to this task is
A. 10   B. 15   C. 24   D. 70

10. Assume that you receive a shipment of 9 boxes of paper towels. Each box contains 6 dozen packages. Each package contains 200 paper towels. The total cost of the shipment of boxes is $64.80. The unit of issue for paper towels is the package.
The unit cost of the paper towels is
A. $.10   B. $.90   C. $1.20   D. $7.20

KEY (CORRECT ANSWERS)

1.	D	6.	D
2.	B	7.	C
3.	A	8.	A
4.	C	9.	A
5.	A	10.	A

3 (#3)

SOLUTIONS TO PROBLEMS

1. Solve for x: 5/60 = x/600. Then, x = 50

2. 960 ÷ 8 = 120 days. Then, 120 – 60 = 60 days

3. Storage area is (175)(140) – (35)(75) – (10)(21) = 21,665 sq.ft.

4. 9 × 9 = 81 sq.in. (81)(10) = 810 sq.in. of tiles cost $3.50. (15ft)(21ft) = (180)(252) = 45,360 sq.in. Now, 45,360 ÷ 810 = 56 boxes. Finally, (56)($3.50) = $196

5. (2ft)(4ft)(4ft) = (24 in)(48 in)(48 in) = 55,296 sq.in. Then, 55,296/27 = 2048 boxes.

6. Balance at end of April 13th is 75 + 50 – 75 = 50
   Balance at end of April 14th is 50 + 0 – 10 = 40
   Balance at end of April 15th is 40 + 25 – 0 = 65

7. (4 1/2)(5) = 224 sq.ft. Then, (22)($0.10) = $2.25 per piece. The cost of 12 pieces is ($2.25)(12) = $27

8. If 10 man-hours are needed for 4 tons, then 200 man-hours are needed for 80 tons. The number of men needed to do the job in 20 hours is 200 ÷ 20 = 10

9. 7 hours = 420 minutes and 420 ÷ 10 = 42.
   Then, (42)(12) = 504 reams transported per day for each laborer. Now, 5000 ÷ 504 ≈ 9.92, which gets rounded up to 10.

10. (9)(72) = 648 package. Then, $64.80 ÷ 648 = $0.10

ARITHMETICAL COMPUTATION AND REASONING
EXAMINATION SECTION
TEST 1

DIRECTIONS: Each question or incomplete statement is followed by several suggested answers or completions. Select the one that BEST answers the question or completes the statement. *PRINT THE LETTER OF THE CORRECT ANSWER IN THE SPACE AT THE RIGHT.*

1. 3/8 less than $40 is
   A. $25   B. $65   C. $15   D. $55

2. 27/64 expressed as a percent is
   A. 40.625%   B. 42.188%   C. 43.750%   D. 45.313%

3. 1/6 more than 36 gross is _____ gross.
   A. 6   B. 48   C. 30   D. 42

4. 15 is 20% of

5. The number which when increased by 1/3 of itself equals 96 is
   A. 128   B. 72   C. 64   D. 32

6. 0.16 3/4 written as percent is
   A. 16 3/4%   B. 16.3/4%   C. .016 3/4%   D. .0016 3/4%

7. 55% of 15 is
   A. 82.5   B. 0.825   C. 0.0825   D. 8.25

8. The number which when decreased by 1/3 of itself equals 96 is
   A. 64   B. 32   C. 128   D. 144

9. A carpenter used a board 15 3/4 ft. long from which 3 footstools were made with sufficient lumber left over for half of another footstool.
   If the lumber cost 24 1/2¢ per foot, the cost of EACH footstool was
   A. $1.54   B. $3.86   C. $1.10   D. $1.08

10. In one year, a luncheonette purchased 1231 gallons of milk for $907.99. The AVERAGE cost per half pint was
    A. $0.046   B. $0.045   C. $0.047   D. $0.044

11. The product of 23 and 9 3/4 is
    A. 191 2/3   B. 224 1/4   C. 213 3/4   D. 32 3/4

12. An order for 345 machine bolts at $4.15 per hundred will cost
    A. $0.1432   B. $1.1432   C. $14.32   D. $143.20

2 (#1)

13. The fractional equivalent of .0625 is 13.____
    A. 1/16   B. 1/15   C. 1/14   D. 1/13

14. The number 0.03125 equals 14.____
    A. 3/64   B. 1/16   C. 1/64   D. 1/32

15. 21.70 divided by 1.75 equals 15.____
    A. 124   B. 12.4   C. 1.24   D. .124

16. The average cost of school lunches for 100 children varied as follows: Monday, $0.285; 16.____
    Tuesday, $0.237; Wednesday, $0.264; Thursday, $0.276; Friday, $0.292.
    The AVERAGE lunch cost
    A. $0.136   B. $0.270   C. $0.135   D. $0.271

17. The cost of 5 dozen eggs at $8.52 per gross is 17.____
    A. $3.50   B. $42.60   C. $3.55   D. $3.74

18. 410.07 less 38.49 equals 18.____
    A. 372.58   B. 371.58   C. 381.58   D. 382.68

19. The cost of 7 3/4 tons of coal at $20.16 per ton is 19.____
    A. $15.12   B. $151.20   C. $141.12   D. $156.24

20. The sum of 90.79, 79.09, 97.90, and 9.97 is 20.____
    A. 277.75   B. 278.56   C. 276.94   D. 277.93

KEY (CORRECT ANSWERS)

1. A   11. B
2. B   12. C
3. D   13. A
4. C   14. D
5. B   15. B

6. A   16. D
7. D   17. C
8. D   18. B
9. C   19. D
10. A   20. A

3 (#1)

SOLUTIONS TO PROBLEMS

1. ($40)(5/8) = $25

2. 27/64 = .421875 ≈ 42.188%

3. (36)(1 1/6) = 42

4. Let x = missing number. Then, 15 = .20x. Solving, x = 75

5. Let x = missing number. Then, x + 1/3 x = 96. Simplifying, 4/3 x = 96. Solving, x = 96 ÷ 4/3 = 72

6. .16 3/4 = 16 3/4% by simply moving the decimal point two places to the right.

7. (.55)(15) = 8.25

8. Let x = missing number. Then, x - 1/3 x = 96. Simplifying, 2/3 x = 96. Solving, x = 96 ÷ 2/3 = 144

9. 15 3/4 ÷ 3 1/2 = 4.5 feet per footstool. The cost of one footstool is ($.245)(4.5) = $1.1025 ≈ $1.10

10. $907.99 ÷ 1231 = $.7376 per gallon. Since there are 16 half-pints in a gallon, the average cost per half-pint is $.7376 ÷ 16 ≈ $.046

11. (23)(9 3/4) = (23)(9.75) = 224.25 or 224 1/4

12. ($4.15)(3.45) = $14.3175 = $14.32

13. .0625 = 625/10,000 = 1/16

14. .03125 = 3125/100,000 = 1/32

15. 21.70 ÷ 1.75 = 12.4

16. The sum of these lunches is $1.354. Then, $1.354 ÷ 5 = $.2708 = $.271

17. $8.52 ÷ 12 = $.71 per dozen. Then, the cost of 5 dozen is ($.71)(5) = $3.55

18. 410.07 - 38.49 = 371.58

19. ($20.16)(7.75) = $156.24

20. 90.79 + 79.09 + 97.90 + 9.97 = 277.75

TEST 2

DIRECTIONS: Each question or incomplete statement is followed by several suggested answers or completions. Select the one that BEST answers the question or completes the statement. *PRINT THE LETTER OF THE CORRECT ANSWER IN THE SPACE AT THE RIGHT.*

1. 1600 is 40% of what number? 1.____
   A. 6400   B. 3200   C. 4000   D. 5600

2. An executive's time card reads: Arrived 9:15 A.M., Left 2:05 P.M. 2.____
   How many hours was he in the office? _____ hours _____ minutes.
   A. 5; 10   B. 4; 50   C. 4; 10   D. 5; 50

3. .4266 times .3333 will have the following number of decimals in the product: 3.____
   A. 8   B. 4   C. 1   D. None of these

4. An office floor is 25 ft. wide by 36 ft. long. 4.____
   To cover this floor with carpet will require _____ square yards.
   A. 100   B. 300   C. 900   D. 25

5. 1/8 of 1% expressed as a decimal is 5.____
   A. .125   B. .0125   C. 1.25   D. .00125

6. $\dfrac{6 \div 4}{6 \times 4}$ equals 6x4 6.____
   A. 1/16   B. 1   C. 1/6   D. 1/4

7. 1/25 of 230 equals 7.____
   A. 92.0   B. 9.20   C. .920   D. 920

8. 4 times 3/8 equals 8.____
   A. 1 3/8   B. 3/32   C. 12.125   D. 1.5

9. 3/4 divided by 4 equals 9.____
   A. 3   B. 3/16   C. 16/3   D. 16

10. 6/7 divided by 2/7 equals 10.____
    A. 6   B. 12/49   C. 3   D. 21

11. The interest on $240 for 90 days ' 6% is 11.____
    A. $4.80   B. $3.40   C. $4.20   D. $3.60

12. 16 2/3% of 1728 is 12.____
    A. 91   B. 288   C. 282   D. 280

13. 6 1/4% of 6400 is 13.____
   A. 2500   B. 410   C. 108   D. 400

14. 12 1/2% of 560 is 14.____
   A. 65   B. 40   C. 50   D. 70

15. 2 yards divided by 3 equals 15.____
   A. 2 feet   B. 1/2 yard   C. 3 yards   D. 3 feet

16. A school has 540 pupils. 45% are boys. How many girls are there in this school? 16.____
   A. 243   B. 297   C. 493   D. 394

17. .1875 is equivalent to 17.____
   A. 18 3/4   B. 75/18   C. 18/75   D. 3/16

18. A kitchen cabinet listed at $42 is sold for $33.60. The discount allowed is 18.____
   A. 10%   B. 15%   C. 20%   D. 30%

19. 3 6/8 divided by 8 1/4 equals 19.____
   A. 9 1/8   B. 12   C. 5/11   D. 243.16

20. An agent sold goods to the amount of $1480. His commission at 5 1/2% was 20.____
   A. $37.50   B. $81.40   C. 76.70   D. $81.10

KEY (CORRECT ANSWERS

1. C   11. D
2. B   12. B
3. A   13. D
4. A   14. D
5. D   15. A

6. A   16. B
7. B   17. D
8. D   18. C
9. B   19. C
10. C   20. B

SOLUTIONS TO PROBLEMS

1. Let x = missing number. Then, 1600 = .40x. Solving, x = 4000
2. 2:05 PM - 9:15 AM = 4 hours 50 minutes
3. The product of two 4-decimal numbers is an 8-decimal number.
4. (25 ft)(36 ft) = 900 sq.ft. = 100 sq.yds.
5. (1/8)(1%) = (.125)(.01) = .00125
6. (6 ÷ 4) ÷ (6 x 4) = 3/2 ÷ 24 = (3/2)(1/24) = (1/16)
7. (1/25)(230) = 9.20
8. (4)(3/8) = 12/8 = 1.5
9. 3/4 ÷ 4 = (3/4)(1/4) = 3/16
10. 6/7 / 2/7 = (6/7)(7/2) = 3
11. ($240)(.06)(90/360) = $3.60
12. (16 2/3%)(1728) = (1/6)(1728) = 288
13. (6 1/4%)(6400) = (1/16)(6400) = 400
14. (12 1/2%)(560) = (1/8)(560) = 70
15. 2 yds ÷ 3 = 2/3 yds = (2/3)(3) = 2 ft.
16. If 45% are boys, then 55% are girls. Thus, (540)(.55) = 297
17. .1875 = 1875/10,000 = 3/16
18. $42 - $33.60 = $8.40.
    The discount is $8.40 ÷ $42 = .20 = 20%
19. 3 6/8 - 8 1/4 = (30/8)(4/33) = 5/11
20. ($1480)(.055) = $81.40

TEST 3

DIRECTIONS: Each question or incomplete statement is followed by several suggested answers or completions. Select the one that BEST answers the question or completes the statement. *PRINT THE LETTER OF THE CORRECT ANSWER IN THE SPACE AT THE RIGHT.*

1. 93.648 divided by 0.4 is

    A. 23.412 B. 234.12 C. 2.3412 D. 2341.2

2. Add 4.3682, .0028, 34., 9.92, and from the sum subtract 1.992. The remainder is

    A. .46299 B. 4.6299 C. 462.99 D. 46.299

3. At $2.88 per gross, three dozen will cost

    A. $8.64 B. $0.96 C. $0.72 D. $11.52

4. 13 times 2.39 times 0.024 equals

    A. 745.68 B. 74.568 C. 7.4568 D. .74568

5. A living room suite is marked $64 less 25 percent. A cash discount of 10 percent is allowed.
   The cash price is

    A. $53.20 B. $47.80 C. $36.00 D. $43.20

6. 1/8 of 1 percent expressed as a decimal is

    A. .125 B. .0125 C. 1.25 D. .00125

7. 16 percent of 482.11 equals

    A. 77.1376 B. 771.4240 C. 7714.2400 D. 7.71424

8. A merchant sold a chair for $60. This was at a profit of 25 percent of what it cost him. The chair cost him

    A. $48 B. $45 C. $15 D. $75

9. Add 5 hours 13 minutes, 3 hours 49 minutes, and 14 minutes. The sum is _____ hours _____ minutes.

    A. 9; 16 B. 9;76 C. 8;16 D. 8;6

10. 89 percent of $482 is

    A. $428.98 B. $472.36 C. $42.90 D. $47.24

11. 200 percent of 800 is

    A. 16 B. 1600 C. 2500 D. 4

12. Add 2 feet 3 inches, 4 feet 11 inches, 8 inches, 6 feet 6 inches. The sum is _____ feet _____ inches.

    A. 12; 4 B. 12; 14 C. 14; 4 D. 14; 28

13. A merchant bought dresses at $15 each and sold them at $20 each. His overhead expenses are 20 percent of cost. His net profit on each dress is

    A. $1
    B. $2
    C. $3
    D. $4

    13._____

14. 0.0325 expressed as a percent is

    A. 325%
    B. 3 1/4%
    C. 32 1/2%
    D. 32.5%

    14._____

15. Add 3/4, 1/8, 1/32, 1/2; and from the sum subtract 4/8. The remainder is

    A. 2/32
    B. 7/8
    C. 29/32
    D. 3/4

    15._____

16. A salesman gets a commission of 4 percent on his sales. If he wants his commission to amount to $40, he will have to sell merchandise totaling

    A. $160
    B. $10
    C. $1,000
    D. $100

    16._____

17. Jones borrowed $225,000 for five years at 3 1/2 percent. The annual interest charge was

    A. $1,575
    B. $1,555
    C. $7,875
    D. $39,375

    17._____

18. A kitchen cabinet listed at $42 is sold for $33.60. The discount allowed is _____ percent.

    A. 10
    B. 15
    C. 20
    D. 30

    18._____

19. The exact number of days from May 5, 2007 to July 1, 2007 is _____ days.

    A. 59
    B. 58
    C. 56
    D. 57

    19._____

20. A dealer sells an article at a loss of 50% of the cost. Based on the selling price, the loss is

    A. 25%
    B. 50%
    C. 100%
    D. none of these

    20._____

KEY (CORRECT ANSWERS)

1.	B	11.	B
2.	D	12.	C
3.	C	13.	B
4.	D	14.	B
5.	D	15.	C
6.	D	16.	C
7.	A	17.	C
8.	A	18.	C
9.	A	19.	D
10.	A	20.	C

SOLUTIONS TO PROBLEMS

1. $93.648 \div .4 = 234.12$

2. $4.368 + .0028 + 34 + 9.92 - 1.992 = 48.291 - 1.992 = 46.299$

3. $2.88 for 12 dozen means $.24 per dozen. Three dozen will cost $(3)(\$.24) = \$.72$

4. $(13)(2.39)(.024) = .74568$

5. $(\$64)(.75)(.90) = \$43.20$

6. $(1/8)(1\%) = (.125)(.01) = .00125$

7. $(.16)(482.11) = 77.1376$

8. Let x = cost. Then, $1.25x = \$60$. Solving, $x = \$48$

9. 5 hrs. 13 min. + 3 hrs. 49 min. + 14 min = 8 hrs. 76 min.

10. $(.89)(\$482) = \$428.98$

11. $200\% = 2$. So, $(200\%)(800) = (2)(800) = 1600$

12. 2 ft. 3 in. + 4 ft. 11 in. + 8 in. + 6 ft. 6 in. + 12 ft. 28 in. = 14 ft. 4 in.

13. Overhead is $(.20)(\$15) = \$3$. The net profit is $\$20 - \$15 - \$3 = \$2$

14. $.0325 = 3.25\% = 3\ 1/4\%$

15. $3/4 + 1/8 + 1/32 + 1/2 - 4/8 = 45/32 - 4/8 = 29/32$

16. Let x = sales. Then, $\$40 = .04x$. Solving, $x = \$1000$

17. Annual interest is $(\$225,000)(.035) \times 1 = 7875$

18. $\$42 - \$33.60 = \$8.40$. Then, $\$8.40 \div \$42 = .20 = 20\%$

19. The number of days left for May, June, July is 26, 30, and 1. Thus, $26 + 30 + 1 = 57$

20. Let x = cost, so that $.50x$ = selling price. The loss is represented by $.50x \div .50x = 1 = 100\%$ on the selling price. (Note: The loss in dollars is $x - .50x = .50x$)

INTERPRETING STATISTICAL DATA GRAPHS, CHARTS AND TABLES
EXAMINATION SECTION
TEST 1

DIRECTIONS: Each question or incomplete statement is followed by several suggested answers or completions. Select the one that BEST answers the question or completes the statement. *PRINT THE LETTER OF THE CORRECT ANSWER IN THE SPACE AT THE RIGHT.*

Questions 1-5.

DIRECTIONS: Questions 1 through 5 are to be answered SOLELY on the basis of the information given below.

LISTING OF PAPER, 100% SULPHITE, FOUND IN STOCKROOM A				
Description	Quantity Ordered by Stockroom A (In dozen reams)	Quantity in Stock Before Delivery (In dozen reams)	Cost Per Ream	Location of Stock in Stockroom
8 1/2"x11" Blue	17	5	$1.88	Bin A7
8 1/2"x11" Buff	8	3	$1.86	Bin A7
8 1/2"x11" Green	11	4	$1.90	Bin B4
8 1/2"x11" Pink	10	4	$1.86	Bin B4
8 1/2"x11" White	80	15	$1.72	Bin A8
8 1/2"x13" White	76	12	$2.04	Bin A8
8 1/2"x14" Blue	7	2	$2.38	Bin A7
8 1/2"x14" Buff	7	3	$2.36	Bin A7
8 1/2"x14" Green	5	2	$2.40	Bin B4
8 1/2"x14" Pink	8	4	$2.36	Bin B4
8 1/2"x14" White	110	28	$2.30	Bin A8
81/2"x14" Yellow	2	1	$2.46	Bin C6

1. How many reams of 8 1/2" x 13" paper will there be in stock if only one-half of the amount ordered is delivered? _____ reams.   1.____

    A. 456　　　B. 600　　　C. 912　　　D. 1,056

2. Suppose all ordered material is delivered.
   The bin that will have the MOST reams of paper is   2.____

    A. A7　　　B. A8　　　C. B4　　　D. C6

91

3. Suppose all ordered material has been delivered.
   What is the APPROXIMATE value of all 8 1/2" x 11" paper which is in Bin B4?

   A. $54 B. $342 C. $396 D. $654

4. How many reams of white paper of all sizes were ordered?
   _____ reams.

   A. 55 B. 266 C. 660 D. 3,192

5. Before any of the orders were delivered, the following requests were filled and removed from the stockroom:
   2 dozen reams 8 1/2" x 11" Blue; 2 dozen reams 8 1/2" x 11" Green; 7 dozen reams 8 1/2" x 11" White; 5 dozen reams 8 1/2" x 13" White; 1 dozen reams 8 1/2" x 14" Green; 13 dozen reams 8 1/2" x 14" White.
   How many reams of paper were left in the stockroom after the above requests were filled?

   A. 30 B. 53 C. 636 D. 996

KEY (CORRECT ANSWERS)

1. B
2. B
3. D
4. D
5. C

TEST 2

Questions 1-4.

DIRECTIONS: Questions 1 through 4 are to be answered SOLELY on the basis of the information given below.

> NUMBER OF SPECIAL ORDERS PICKED AND PACKED EACH DAY DURING WEEK
> Stockman A - Monday 20; Tuesday 20; Wednesday. 25;
> Thursday. 30; Friday 30
> Stockman B - Monday 25; Tuesday 30; Wednesday 35;
> Thursday 20; Friday 35
> Stockman C - Monday 15; Tuesday 20; Wednesday 25;
> Thursday 30; Friday 30
> Stockman D - Monday 30; Tuesday 35; Wednesday 40;
> Thursday 35; Friday 40

1. Which stockman picked and packed a total of exactly 120 special orders during the week?
   Stockman

   A. A B. B C. C D. D

2. The stockman who picked and packed the LEAST number of special orders on Thursday is Stockman

   A. A B. B C. C D. D

3. The total number of special orders picked and packed during the week by all four stockmen is

   A. 125 B. 460 C. 560 D. 570

4. By what percentage did the number of orders picked and packed by Stockman C on Friday exceed the number of orders picked and packed by Stockman C on Monday?

   A. 15% B. 30% C. 100% D. 200%

KEY (CORRECT ANSWERS)

1. C
2. B
3. D
4. C

TEST 3

Questions 1-6.

DIRECTIONS: Questions 1 through 6 are to be answered SOLELY on the basis of the information given in the table below.

RECORD OF INCOMING FREIGHT SHIPMENTS

Date Received	Purchase Order No.	AMOUNT Prepaid	AMOUNT To Be Collected	Shipper	No. of Items	Weight	Shippers' Catalog No.
1/7	9616	$15.10		Harding Grove Equip.	14	170	28
1/12	3388		$ 2.00	People's Paper, Inc.	10	50	091
1/12	8333		$106.19	Falls Office Supply	25	2,500	701
2/2	7126		$ 9.00	Leigh Foods	175	4,000	47
2/13	4964		$ 3.09	McBride Paper Co.	14	75	83
4/13	3380	$14.09		Central Hardware	14	1,750	019
4/30	7261		$ 6.90	Northwestern Foods	121	2,100	13
5/12	9166	$10.50		Harding Grove Equipment	15	50	36
5/17	6949		$ 4.19	Black's Paper Co.	40	65	743
5/31	6691		$ 20.00	Central Hardware	16	600	563
6/30	5388	$ 9.75		Harding Grove Equip.	15	15	420
6/30	8308		$ 22.50	Falls Office Supply	19	290	97
8/23	8553		$ 4.90	Tremont Paper, Inc.	75	570	36
9/12	5338	$ 6.91		Northeast Hardware	51	901	071
10/15	6196	$12.00		Mobray Hardware	60	786	131

1. What is the purchase order number for the Harding Grove equipment shipment that was received on 5/12?

    A. 9166 B. 5388 C. 9616 D. 6691

2. All items that cost less than five dollars ($5.00) came from shippers of

    A. paper
    B. foods
    C. hardware
    D. office supplies

2 (#3)

3. All items listed in the above table were delivered by   3.____
   A. U.S. Mail   B. freight
   C. air express   D. ship

4. On what date was the LARGEST number of items received?   4.____
   A. 2/2   B. 2/13   C. 4/30   D. 5/17

5. If all items shipped by Falls Office Supply on 1/12 were of equal weight, how much did   5.____
   each item weigh? _____ lbs.
   A. 10   B. 25   C. 100   D. 250

6. If the names of the shippers were put in alphabetical order, which of the following should   6.____
   be put AFTER McBride Paper Company?
   A. Northeast Hardware   B. Leigh Foods
   C. Northwestern Foods   D. Mobray Hardware

KEY (CORRECT ANSWERS)

1. A
2. A
3. B
4. A
5. C
6. D

TEST 4

Questions 1-6.

DIRECTIONS: Questions 1 through 6 are to be answered SOLELY on the basis of the information contained in the chart below, which shows the number of requisitions filled by Storeroom A during each month of 2018.

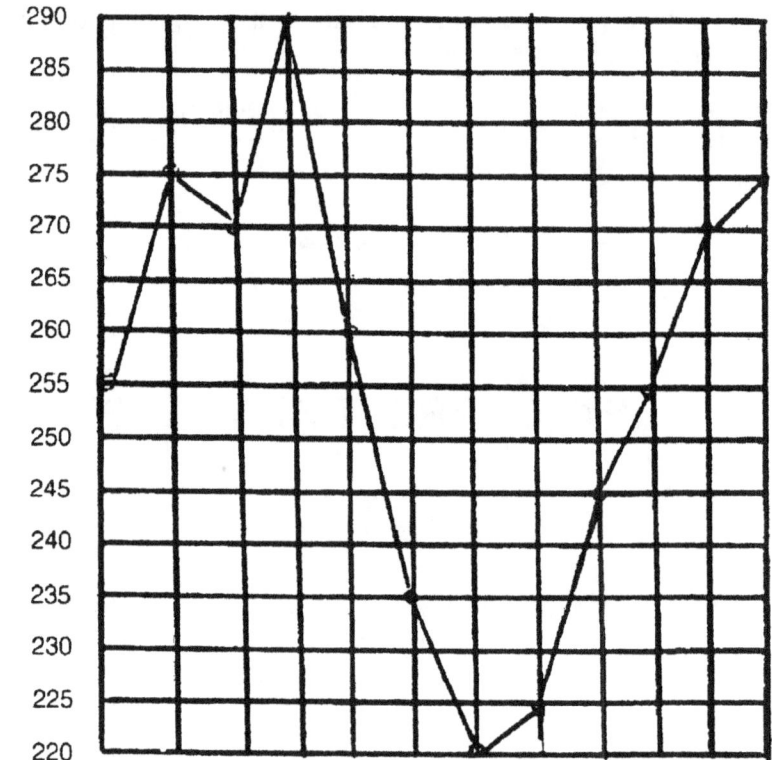

1. According to the above chart, the average number of requisitions handled per month by Storeroom A during the first six months is MOST NEARLY

   A. 250   B. 260   C. 270   D. 280

2. It is expected that the number of requisitions Storeroom A will handle in 2019 will be 10 percent more than it handled in 2018.
   The number of requisitions Storeroom A is expected to handle during the year is

   A. 2,763   B. 3,070   C. 3,377   D. 3,440

3. The month during which the number of requisitions handled showed the GREATEST decrease from the previous month was

   A. April   B. May   C. June   D. July

4. During May, there were 3 clerks assigned to Storeroom A. One man went on vacation for the month of June and was not replaced.
   The number of additional orders handled by each man working in June over the number of orders handled per man in May was MOST NEARLY

   A. 20   B. 27   C. 32   D. 36

5. During June, July, and August, 8 percent of the requisitions handled were rush orders. The number of rush orders handled during these three months is MOST NEARLY

   A. 55   B. 60   C. 65   D. 70

6. During November, there were three clerks assigned to Storeroom A.
   If one handled 95 requisitions and another handled 85 requisitions, the number of requisitions handled by the third clerk was

   A. 70   B. 80   C. 90   D. 100

KEY (CORRECT ANSWERS)

1. B
2. C
3. B
4. C
5. A
6. C

TEST 5

Questions 1-10.

DIRECTIONS: Questions 1 through 10 are to be answered SOLELY on the basis of the information given in the table below.

TABLE OF INFORMATION ABOUT GARDEN HOSE ON HAND

Commodity Index Number	Kind & Diameter of Hose (in inches)	Number of Feet Per Roll	Weight Per Roll lbs.	Weight Per Roll ozs.	Cost Per Roll	Number of Rolls on Hand
SL 14171	Plastic, 3/4"	25	6	5	$5.90	20
SL 14172	Plastic, 3/4"	50	12	5	9.90	50
SL 14271	Plastic, 5/8"	25	4	7	4.40	40
SL 14272	Plastic, 5/8"	50	8	10	7.40	50
SL 14273	Plastic, 5/8"	75	13	0	10.40	50
SL 14274	Plastic, 5/8"	100	17	0	13.40	100
SL 24171	Rubber, Reinforced, 3/4"	25	9	3	8.90	20
SL 24172	Rubber, Reinforced, 3/4"	50	18	0	14.90	10
SL 24271	Rubber, Reinforced, 5/8"	25	6	2	6.20	40
SL 24272	Rubber, Reinforced, 5/8"	50	12	2	10.90	40
SL 24273	Rubber, Reinforced, 5/8"	75	18	0	15.20	60
SL 24274	Rubber, Reinforced, 5/8"	100	24	0	19.90	100

1. The total number of 25 foot rolls of all types of garden hose currently on hand is

    A. 120   B. 180   C. 220   D. 400

2. The total weight of one roll each of SL 14172, SL 14273, SL 24271, and SL 24274 is _____ lbs. _____ oz.

    A. 49; 7   B. 51; 7   C. 55; 7   D. 61; 7

3. The total weight of all of the 25 foot rolls of rubber, reinforced, 5/8" garden hose on hand is _____ lbs.

    A. 175   B. 240   C. 245   D. 485

4. An order for 10 rolls of SL 14271, 17 rolls of SL 14274, and 22 rolls of SL 24271 will MOST NEARLY weigh _____ lbs.

    A. 333   B. 423   C. 468   D. 472

5. The total cost of 12 rolls of 100 foot plastic, 5/8" garden hose is

    A. $124.80   B. $134.00   C. $160.80   D. $238.80

6. Assume that from the 40 rolls of SL 24272 and the 100 rolls of SL 24274 you ship one order of 10 rolls of SL 24272 and one order of 50 rolls of SL 24274.
   The total cost of all of the SL 24272 and the SL 24274 garden hose still on hand after filling these orders is

   A. $479   B. $1,104   C. $1,322   D. $1,451

7. Assume that 15% of all the 100 foot rolls of plastic garden hose and rubber reinforced garden hose are found defective.
   Then, the total cost of the defective hose is

   A. $199.00   B. $298.00   C. $333.00   D. $499.50

8. The stock on hand of which one of the following sizes and types of garden hose has the GREATEST total cost?

   A. SL 14171   B. SL 14271   C. SL 24171   D. SL 24172

9. If 3/4" plastic garden hose is taken from the 50 foot rolls, then the cost of one foot of such hose is MOST NEARLY

   A. 20¢   B. 23¢   C. 26¢   D. 29¢

10. If it takes one worker one hour to inspect 20 rolls of garden hose for defects, the LEAST amount of time it will take two workers to inspect ALL the rolls of garden hose in stock is _____ hours _____ minutes.

    A. 14; 30   B. 15; 50   C. 24; 10   D. 29; 0

KEY (CORRECT ANSWERS)

1. A   6. C
2. C   7. D
3. C   8. C
4. C   9. A
5. C   10. A

NAME AND NUMBER CHECKING
EXAMINATION SECTION
TEST 1

DIRECTIONS: This test is designed to measure your speed/and accuracy. You are urged to work both quickly and accurately and to do correctly as many lists as you can in the time allowed. The test consists of lists or pairs of names and numbers. Count the number of IDENTICAL pairs in each list. Then, select the correct number, 1, 2, 3, 4, 5, and indicate your choice in the space at the right. Two sample questions are presented for your guidance, together with the correct solutions.

SAMPLE LIST A
Adelphi College – Adelphia College
Braxton Corp – Braxeton Corp.
Wassaic State School – Wassaic State School
Central Islip State Hospital – Central Isllip State Hospital
Greenwich House – Greenwich House

NOTE: There are only two correct pairs—Wassaic State School and Greenwich House. Therefore, the CORRECT answer is 2.

SAMPLE LIST B
78453694 – 78453684
784530 – 784530
533 – 534
67845 – 67845
2368745 – 2368755

NOTE: There are only two correct pairs—784530 and 67845. Therefore, the CORRECT answer is 2.

LIST 1   1.____
    Diagnostic Clinic   – Diagnostic Clinic
    Yorkville Health   – Yorkville Health
    Meinhard Clinic   – Meinhart Clinic
    Corlears Clinic   – Carlears Clinic
    Tremont Diagnostic   – Tremont Diagnostic

LIST 2   2.____
    73526   – 73526
    7283627198   – 7283627198
    627   – 637
    728352617283   – 7283526178282
    6281   – 6281

2 (#1)

LIST 3   3._____
    Jefferson Clinic — Jeffersen Clinic
    Mott Haven Center — Mott Havan Center
    Bronx Hospital — Bronx Hospital
    Montefiore Hospital — Montifeore Hospital
    Beth Isreal Hospital — Beth Israel Hospital

LIST 4   4._____
    936271826 — 936371826
    5271 — 5291
    82637192037 — 82637192037
    527182 — 5271882
    726354256 — 72635456

LIST 5   5._____
    Trinity Hospital — Trinity Hospital
    Central Harlem — Centrel Harlem
    St. Luke's Hospital — St. Lukes' Hospital
    Mt. Sinai Hospital — Mt. Sinia Hospital
    N.Y. Dispensery — N.Y. Dispensary

LIST 6   6._____
    725361552637 — 725361555637
    7526378 — 7526377
    6975 — 6975
    82637481028 — 82637481028
    3427 — 3429

LIST 7   7._____
    Misericordia Hospital — Miseracordia Hospital
    Lebonan Hospital — Lebanon Hospital
    Gouverneur Hospital — Gouverner Hospital
    German Polyclinic — German Policlinic
    French Hospital — French Hospital

LIST 8   8._____
    8277364933251 — 827364933351
    63728 — 63728
    367281 — 367281
    62733846273 — 6273846293
    62836 — 6283

LIST 9   9._____
    King's County Hospital — Kings County Hospital
    St. Johns Long Island — St. John's Long Island
    Bellevue Hospital — Bellvue Hospital
    Beth David Hospital — Beth David Hospital
    Samaritan Hospital — Samariton Hospital

3 (#1)

LIST 10   10.____
    62836454   – 62836455
    42738267   – 42738369
    573829   – 573829
    738291627874   – 738291627874
    725   - 735

LIST 11   11.____
    Bloomingdal Clinic   – Bloomingdale Clinic
    Communitty Hospital   – Community Hospital
    Metroplitan Hospital   – Metropoliton Hospital
    Lenox Hill Hospital   – Lonex Hill Hospital
    Lincoln Hospital   – Lincoln Hospital

LIST 12   12.____
    6283364728   – 6283648
    627385   – 627383
    54283902   – 54283602
    63354   – 63354
    7283562781   - 7283562781

LIST 13   13.____
    Sydenham Hospital   – Sydanham Hospital
    Roosevalt Hospital   – Roosevelt Hospital
    Vanderbilt Clinic   – Vanderbild Clinic
    Women's Hospital   – Woman's Hospital
    Flushing Hospital   – Flushing Hospital

LIST 14   14.____
    62738   – 62738
    727355542321   – 72735542321
    263849332   – 263849332
    262837   – 263837
    47382912   - 47382922

LIST 15   15.____
    Episcopal Hospital   – Episcapal Hospital
    Flower Hospital   – Flouer Hospital
    Stuyvesent Clinic   – Stuyvesant Clinic
    Jamaica Clinic   – Jamaica Clinic
    Ridgwood Clinic   – Ridgewood Clinic

LIST 16   16.____
    628367299   – 628367399
    111   – 111
    118293304829   – 1182839489
    4448   – 4448
    333693678   - 333693678

4 (#1)

LIST 17   17.____
    Arietta Crane Farm   – Areitta Crane Farm
    Bikur Chilim Home   – Bikur Chilom Home
    Burke Foundation   – Burke Foundation
    Blythedale Home   – Blythdale Home
    Campbell Cottages   – Cambell Cottages

LIST 18   18.____
    32123   – 32132
    273893326783   – 27389326783
    473829   – 473829
    7382937   – 7383937
    3628890122332   - 36289012332

LIST 19   19.____
    Caraline Rest   – Caroline Rest
    Loreto Rest   – Loretto Rest
    Edgewater Creche   – Edgwater Creche
    Holiday Farm   – Holiday Farm
    House of St. Giles   – House of st. Giles

LIST 20   20.____
    557286777   – 55728677
    3678902   – 3678892
    1567839   – 1567839
    7865434712   – 7865344712
    9927382   - 9927382

LIST 21   21.____
    Isabella Home   – Isabela Home
    James A. Moore Home   – James A. More Home
    The Robin's Nest   – The Roben's Nest
    Pelham Home   – Pelam Home
    St. Eleanora's Home   – St. Eleanora's Home

LIST 22   22.____
    273648293048   – 273648293048
    334   – 334
    7362536478   – 7362536478
    7362819273   – 7362819273
    7362   - 7363

LIST 23   23.____
    St. Pheobe's Mission   – St. Phebe's Mission
    Seaside Home   – Seaside Home
    Speedwell Society   – Speedwell Society
    Valeria Home   – Valera Home
    Wiltwyck   - Wildwyck

5 (#1)

LIST 24
    63728   – 63738
    63728192736   – 63728192738
    428   – 458
    62738291527   – 62738291529
    63728192   - 63728192

24.____

LIST 25
    McGaffin   – McGafin
    David Ardslee   – David Ardslee
    Axton Supply   – Axeton Supply Co
    Alice Russell   – Alice Russell
    Dobson Mfg. Co.   – Dobsen Mfg. Co.

25.____

KEY (CORRECT ANSWERS)

1.	3	11.	1
2.	3	12.	2
3.	1	13.	1
4.	1	14.	2
5.	1	15.	1
6.	2	16.	3
7.	1	17.	1
8.	2	18.	1
9.	1	19.	1
10.	2	20.	2

21.	1
22.	4
23.	2
24.	1
25.	2

TEST 2

DIRECTIONS: This test is designed to measure your speed/and accuracy. You are urged to work both quickly and accurately and to do correctly as many lists as you can in the time allowed. The test consists of lists or pairs of names and numbers. Count the number of IDENTICAL pairs in each list. Then, select the correct number, 1, 2, 3, 4, 5, and indicate your choice in the space at the right.

LIST 1
    82637381028   – 82637281028
    928   – 928
    72937281028   – 72937281028
    7362   – 7362
    927382615   – 927382615

1.____

LIST 2
    Albee Theatre   – Albee Theatre
    Lapland Lumber Co.   – Laplund Lumber Co.
    Adelphi College   – Adelphi College
    Jones & Son Inc.   – Jones & Sons Inc.
    S.W. Ponds Co.   – S.W. Ponds Co.

2.____

LIST 3
    85345   – 85345
    895643278   – 895643277
    726352   – 726353
    632685   – 632685
    7263524   – 7236524

3.____

LIST 4
    Eagle Library   – Eagle Library
    Dodge Ltd.   – Dodge Co.
    Stromberg Carlson   – Stromberg Carlsen
    Clairice Ling   – Clairice Linng
    Mason Book Co.   – Matson Book Co.

4.____

LIST 5
    66273   – 66273
    629   – 629
    7382517283   – 7382517283
    637281   – 639281
    2738261   – 2788261

5.____

LIST 6
    Robert MacColl   – Robert McColl
    Buick Motor   – Buck Motors
    Murray Bay & Co. Ltd.   – Murray Bay Co. Ltd.
    L.T. Ltyle   – L.T. Lyttle
    A.S. Landas   – A.S. Landas

6.____

2 (#2)

LIST 7   7.____
   6271526374890   – 627152637490
   73526189   – 73526189
   5372   – 5392
   637281142   – 63728124
   4783946   – 4783046

LIST 8   8.____
   Tyndall Burke   – Tyndell Burke
   W. Briehl   – W. Briehl
   Burritt Publishing Co.   – Buritt Publishing Co.
   Frederick Breyer & Co.   – Frederick Breyer Co.
   Bailey Buulard   – Bailey Bullard

LIST 9   9.____
   634   – 634
   16837   – 163837
   273892223678   – 27389223678
   527182   – 527782
   3628901223   – 3629002223

LIST 10   10.____
   Ernest Boas   – Ernest Boas
   Rankin Barne   – Rankin Barnes
   Edward Appley   – Edward Appely
   Camel   – Camel
   Caiger Food Co.   – Caiger Food Co.

LIST 11   11.____
   6273   – 6273
   322   – 332
   15672839   – 15672839
   63728192637   – 63728192639
   738   – 738

LIST 12   12.____
   Wells Fargo Co.   – Wells Fargo Co.
   W.D. Brett   – W.D. Britt
   Tassco Co.   – Tassko Co.
   Republic Mills   – Republic Mill
   R.W. Burnham   – R.W. Burhnam

LIST 13   13.____
   7253529152   – 7283529152
   6283   – 6383
   52839102738   – 5283910238
   308   – 398
   82637201927   – 8263720127

3 (#2)

LIST 14   14.____
    Schumacker Co.   – Shumacker Co.
    C.H. Caiger   – C.H. Caiger
    Abraham Strauss   – Abram Straus
    B.F. Boettjer   – B.F. Boettijer
    Cut-Rate Store   – Cut-Rate Stores

LIST 15   15.____
    15273826   – 15273826
    72537   – 73537
    726391027384   – 62639107384
    637389   – 627399
    725382910   – 725382910

LIST 16   16.____
    Hixby Ltd.   – Hixby Lt'd.
    S. Reiner   – S. Riener
    Reynard Co.   – Reynord Co.
    Esso Gassoline Co.   – Esso Gasolene Co.
    Belle Brock   – Belle Brock

LIST 17   17.____
    7245   – 7245
    819263728192   – 819263728172
    682537289   – 682537298
    789   – 789
    82936542891   – 82936542891

LIST 18   18.____
    Joseph Cartwright   – Joseph Cartwrite
    Foote Food Co.   – Foot Food Co.
    Weiman & Held   – Weiman & Held
    Sanderson Shoe Co.   – Sandersen Shoe Co.
    A.M. Byrne   – A.N. Byrne

LIST 19   19.____
    4738267   – 4738277
    63728   – 63729
    6283628901   – 6283628991
    918264   – 918264
    263728192037   – 2637728192073

LIST 20   20.____
    Exray Laboratories   – Exray Labratories
    Curley Toy Co.   – Curly Toy Co.
    J. Lauer & Cross   – J. Laeur & Cross
    Mireco Brands   – Mireco Brands
    Sandor Lorand   – Sandor Larand

4 (#2)

LIST 21 21.____
    607   – 609
    6405   – 6403
    976   – 996
    101267   – 101267
    2065432   – 20965432

LIST 22 22.____
    John Macy & Sons   – John Macy & Son
    Venus Pencil Co.   – Venus Pencil Co.
    Nell McGinnis   – Nell McGinnis
    McCutcheon & Co.   – McCutcheon & Co.
    Sun-Tan Oil   – Sun-Tan Oil

LIST 23 23.____
    703345700   – 703345700
    46754   – 466754
    3367490   – 3367490
    3379   – 3778
    47384   – 47394

LIST 24 24.____
    arthritis   – arthritis
    asthma   – asthma
    endocrine   – endocrene
    gastro-enterological – gastrol-enteralogical
    orthopedic   – orthopedic

LIST 25 25.____
    743829432   – 743828432
    998   – 998
    732816253902   – 732816252902
    46829   – 46830
    7439120249   – 7439210249

KEY (CORRECT ANSWERS)

1.	4	11.	3
2.	3	12.	1
3.	2	13.	1
4.	1	14.	1
5.	2	15.	2
6.	1	16.	1
7.	2	17.	3
8.	1	18.	1
9.	1	19.	1
10.	3	20.	1

21. 1
22. 4
23. 2
24. 3
25. 1

NAME AND NUMBER COMPARISONS

COMMENTARY

This test seeks to measure your ability and disposition to do a job carefully and accurately, your attention to exactness and preciseness of detail, your alertness and versatility in discerning similarities and differences between things, and your power in systematically handling written language symbols.

It is actually a test of your ability to do academic and/or clerical work, using the basic elements of verbal (qualitative) and mathematical (quantitative) learning—words and numbers.

EXAMINATION SECTION

TEST 1

DIRECTIONS: In each line across the page there are three names or numbers that are much alike. Compare the three names or numbers and decide which ones are exactly alike. *PRINT IN THE SPACE AT THE RIGHT THE LETTER:*
  A. if all THREE names or numbers are exactly alike
  B. if only the FIRST and SECOND names or numbers are ALIKE
  C. if only the FIRST and THIRD names or numbers are alike
  D. if only the SECOND or THIRD names or numbers are alike
  E. if ALL THREE names or numbers are DIFFERENT

1.	Davis Hazen	David Hozen	David Hazen	1.____
2.	Lois Appel	Lois Appel	Lois Apfel	2.____
3.	June Allan	Jane Allan	Jane Allan	3.____
4.	10235	10235	10235	4.____
5.	32614	32164	32614	5.____

TEST 2

1.	2395890	2395890	2395890	1.____
2.	1926341	1926347	1926314	2.____
3.	E. Owens McVey	E. Owen McVey	E. Owen McVay	3.____
4.	Emily Neal Rouse	Emily Neal Rowse	Emily Neal Rowse	4.____
5.	H. Merritt Audubon	H. Merriott Audubon	H. Merritt Audubon	5.____

TEST 3

1.	6219354	6219354	6219354	1.____
2.	231793	2312793	2312793	2.____
3.	1065407	1065407	1065047	3.____
4.	Francis Ransdell	Frances Ramsdell	Francis Ramsdell	4.____
5.	Cornelius Detwiler	Cornelius Detwiler	Cornelius Detwiler	5.____

TEST 4

1.	6452054	6452564	6542054	1.____
2.	8501268	8501268	8501286	2.____
3.	Ella Burk Newham	Ella Burk Newnham	Elena Burk Newnham	3.____
4.	Jno. K. Ravencroft	Jno. H. Ravencroft	Jno. H. Ravencoft	4.____
5.	Martin Wills Pullen	Martin Wills Pulen	Martin Wills Pullen	5.____

TEST 5

1.	3457988	3457986	3457986	1.____
2.	4695682	4695862	4695682	2.____
3.	Stricklund Kaneydy	Sticklund Kanedy	Stricklund Kanedy	3.____
4.	Joy Harlor Witner	Joy Harloe Witner	Joy Harloe Witner	4.____
5.	R.M.O. Uberroth	R.M.O. Uberroth	R.N.O. Uberroth	5.____

TEST 6

1.	1592514	1592574	1592574	1.____
2.	2010202	2010202	2010220	2.____
3.	6177396	6177936	6177396	3.____
4.	Drusilla S. Ridgeley	Drusilla S. Ridgeley	Drusilla S. Ridgeley	4.____
5.	Andrei I. Tooumantzev	Andrei I. Tourmantzev	Andrei I. Toumantzov	5.____

TEST 7

1.	5261383	5261383	5261338	1.____
2.	8125690	8126690	8125609	2.____
3.	W.E. Johnston	W.E. Johnson	W.E. Johnson	3.____
4.	Vergil L. Muller	Vergil L. Muller	Vergil L. Muller	4.____
5.	Atherton R. Warde	Asheton R. Warde	Atherton P. Warde	5.____

TEST 8

1.	013469.5	023469.5	02346.95	1.____
2.	33376	333766	333766	2.____
3.	Ling-Temco-Vought	Ling-Tenco-Vought	Ling-Temco Vought	3.____
4.	Lorilard Corp.	Lorillard Corp.	Lorrilard Corp.	4.____
5.	American Agronomics Corporation	American Agronomics Corporation	American Agronomic Corporation	5.____

TEST 9

1.	436592864	436592864	436592864	1.____
2.	197765123	197755123	197755123	2.____
3.	Dewaay Cortvriendt International S.A.	Deway Cortvriendt International S.A.	Deway Corturiendt International S.A.	3.____
4.	Crédit Lyonnais	Crèdit Lyonnais	Crèdit Lyonais	4.____
5.	Algemene Bank Nederland N.V.	Algamene Bank Nederland N.V.	Algemene Bank Naderland N.V.	5.____

TEST 10

1.	00032572	0.0032572	00032522	1.____
2.	399745	399745	398745	2.____
3.	Banca Privata Finanziaria S.p.A.	Banca Privata Finanzaria S.P.A.	Banca Privata Finanziaria S.P.A.	3.____
4.	Eastman Dillon, Union Securities & Co.	Eastman Dillon, Union Securities Co.	Eastman Dillon, Union Securities & Co.	4.____
5.	Arnhold and S. Bleichroeder, Inc.	Arnhold & S. Bleichroeder, Inc.	Arnold and S. Bleichroeder, Inc.	5.____

TEST 11

DIRECTIONS: Answer the questions below on the basis of the following instructions: For each such numbered set of names, addresses, and numbers listed in Columns I and II, select your answer from the following options:
- A. The names in Columns I and II are different
- B. The addresses in Columns I and II are different
- C. The numbers in Columns I and II are different
- D. The names, addresses and numbers are identical

1. Francis Jones
   62 Stately Avenue
   96-12446

   Francis Jones
   62 Stately Avenue
   96-21446

   1.____

2. Julio Montez
   19 Ponderosa Road
   56-73161

   Julio Montez
   19 Ponderosa Road
   56-71361

   2.____

3. Mary Mitchell
   2314 Melbourne Drive
   68-92172

   Mary Mitchell
   2314 Melbourne Drive
   68-92172

   3.____

4. Harry Patterson
   25 Dunne Street
   14-33430

   Harry Patterson
   25 Dunne Street
   14-34330

   4.____

5. Patrick Murphy
   171 West Hosmer Street
   93-81214

   Patrick Murphy
   171 West Hosmer Street
   93-18214

   5.____

TEST 12

1. August Schultz
   816 St. Clair Avenue
   53-40149

   August Schultz
   816 St. Claire Avenue
   53-40149

   1.____

2. George Taft
   72 Runnymede Street
   47-04033

   George Taft
   72 Runnymede Street
   47-04023

   2.____

3. Angus Henderson
   1418 Madison Street
   81-76375

   Angus Henderson
   1418 Madison Street
   81-76375

   3.____

4. Carolyn Mazur
   12 Rivenlew Road
   38-99615

   Carolyn Mazur
   12 Rivervane Road
   38-99615

   4.____

5. Adele Russell
   1725 Lansing Lane
   72-91962

   Adela Russell
   1725 Lansing Lane
   72-91962

   5.____

TEST 13

DIRECTIONS: The following questions are based on the instructions given below. In each of the following questions, the 3-line name and address in Column I is the master-list entry, and the 3-line entry in Column II is the information to be checked against the master list.
If there is one line that is NOT exactly alike, mark your answer A.
If there are two lines NOT exactly alike, mark your answer B.
If there are three lines NOT exactly alike, mark your answer C.
If the lines ALL are exactly alike, mark your answer D.

1. Jerome A. Jackson
   1243 14th Avenue
   New York, N.Y. 10023

   Jerome A. Johnson
   1234 14th Avenue
   New York, N.Y. 10023

   1.____

2. Sophie Strachtheim
   33-28 Connecticut Ave.
   Far Rockaway, N.Y. 11697

   Sophie Strachtheim
   33-28 Connecticut Ave.
   Far Rockaway, N.Y. 11697

   2.____

3. Elisabeth NT. Gorrell
   256 Exchange St
   New York, N.Y. 10013

   Elizabeth NT. Correll
   256 Exchange St.
   New York, N.Y. 10013

   3.____

4. Maria J. Gonzalez
   7516 E. Sheepshead Rd.
   Brooklyn, N.Y. 11240

   Maria J. Gonzalez
   7516 N. Shepshead Rd.
   Brooklyn, N.Y. 11240

   4.____

5. Leslie B. Brautenweiler
   21-57A Seller Terr.
   Flushing, N.Y. 11367

   Leslie B. Brautenwieler
   21-75ASeiler Terr.
   Flushing, N.J. 11367

   5.____

KEY (CORRECT ANSWERS)

TEST 1	TEST 2	TEST 3	TEST 4	TEST 5	TEST 6	TEST 7
1. E	1. A	1. A	1. E	1. D	1. D	1. B
2. B	2. E	2. A	2. B	2. C	2. B	2. E
3. D	3. E	3. B	3. E	3. E	3. C	3. D
4. A	4. D	4. E	4. E	4. D	4. A	4. A
5. C	5. C	5. A	5. C	5. B	5. E	5. E

TEST 8	TEST 9	TEST 10	TEST 11	TEST 12	TEST 13
1. E	1. A	1. E	1. C	1. B	1. B
2. D	2. D	2. B	2. C	2. C	2. D
3. E	3. E	3. E	3. D	3. D	3. A
4. E	4. E	4. C	4. C	4. B	4. A
5. B	5. E	5. E	5. C	5. A	5. C

GLOSSARY OF SHIPPING TERMS AND ABBREVIATIONS

A

a.a.x - Against all risks
ADDRESS - A particular street address (not a U.S. Post Office Box Number), which must include the Post Office Zip Code.
a.d. - After date.
AD. VAL. - According to value (Ad Valorem).
AD VALOREM - A freight rate set at a certain percentage of the value of an article is known as an ad valorem rate.
ANY QUANTITY - Rates are applicable regardless of quantity or weight.
A.1 - First class condition.
AQ - Any quantity.
AVDP. - Avoirdupois.

B

B&SG - Browne & Sharpe gauge
bbl. - Barrel.
B.D.I. - Both dates inclusive
B/E - Bill of exchange.
B/L - Bill of lading.
B.O. - Bad order; Buyer's option.
B/P - Bills payable.
bu. - Bushel.
BULK CARRIER - A bulk carrier is a vessel engaged in the carriage of such bulk commodities as petroleum, grain, or ores which are not packaged, bundled, bottled, or otherwise packed.
BWG- Birmingham wire gauge
bx. - Box.

C

C&F - Cost and freight; the same as c.i.f., except that insurance
is arranged by the buyer.
c.c. - Current cost.
c.f. - Cubic foot.
c.i. - Cost and insurance.
c/i-Certificate of insurance.
CIF - Cost, insurance, and freight: a price quotation under which the exporter quotes a price that includes prepayment of freight charges and insurance to an agreed destination
c.i.f.& e. - Cost, insurance, freight & exchange.
C.O.D. - Cash on delivery; Collection on delivery.
C.O.S. - Cash on shipment.
C.R. – Carrier's risk.
c.t.l.o. - Constructive total loss only. cu. ft. - Cubic feet.
cwt. - Hundredweight.

D

D.A. - Documents for acceptance.
D/A - Days after acceptance.
DAT - Dangerous articles tariff.
d/b/a - Doing business as.
D.D. - Demand draft.
D/D - Date draft
d.d.e. - Dispatch discharging only.

DEFERRED REBATE - A deferred rebate is the return of a portion of the freight charges by a carrier or a conference to a shipper in exchange for the shipper giving all or most of his shipments to the carrier or conference over a specified period of time (usually six months). Payment of the rebate is deferred for a further similar period, during which the shipper must continue to give all or most of his shipments to the rebating carrier or conference. The shipper thus earns a further rebate which will not, however, be paid without an additional period of exclusive or almost exclusive patronage with the carrier or conference. In this way, the shipper becomes tied to the rebating carrier or conference. Although the deferred rebate system is illegal in U.S. foreign commerce, it generally is accepted in the ocean trade between foreign countries.

DENSITY - Density means pounds per cubic foot.

The cubage of loose articles or pieces, or packaged articles of a rectangular, elliptical or square shape on one plane shall be determined by multiplying the greatest straight line dimensions of length, width and depth in inches, including all projections, and dividing the total by 1728 (to obtain cubic feet). The density is the weight of the article divided by the cubic feet thus obtained.

d.l.o. - Dispatch loading only.
dm. - Decimeter.
DM. - Dekameter.
DOT - Department of Transportation.
D.P. - Documents for payment.
d.p. - Direct port.
D/S - Days after sight.
d.w. - Deadweight (tons of 2240 lbs.).
d.w.c. - Deadweight for cargo.

E

E.A.O.N. - Expect as otherwise noted.
E.&.O.E. - Errors and omissions excepted.
E.E. - Errors excepted.
e.g. - For example.
est. - Estimated
est. wt. - Estimated weight.
et.al. - And others

F

f.a.c. - Fast as you can.
FAS - Free along side (vessel): a price quotation under which the exporter quotes a price that includes delivery of the goods to the vessel's side and within reach of its loading tackle. Subsequent risks and expenses are for the account of the buyer.
f.d. - Free discharge.
f.i.o. - Free in and out.
f.i.w. - Free in wagon.
FINISHED - Wooden articles that have passed the state of manufacture "in the white."
   (See IN THE WHITE)
F.M. - Fine measurement.
fms. - Fathoms.
FOB - Free on board (vessel) a price quotation under which the exporter quotes a price that includes delivery of the goods on board the vessel. Subsequent risks and expenses are for the account of the buyer. The term FOB may also be used in conjunction with an inland shipping point in the country of exportation or an inland point in the country of destination. This means that the expenses up to the point specified are for the account of the seller.

FOLDED - An article folded in such a manner as to reduce its bulk 33 1/3% from its normal shipping cubage when not folded.

FOLDED FLAT - An article folded in such a manner as to reduce its bulk 66 2/3% from its normal shipping cubage when not folded.

f.o.r. - Free on rail.

f.r.&c.c. - Free on riot & civil commotion.

ft. - Foot.

G

GAUGE - Where tariffs refer to gauge, they mean the U.S. standard Gauge for determining thickness of sheet or plate steel: Browne & Sharpe Gauge for rods and sheets of aluminum copper, brass and bronze; U. S. Steel Wire Gauge for iron and steel wire.

gm. - Gram.

G.T. - Gross ton.

H

hf. - Half.

hhd. - Hogshead.

ht. - Height.

I

ICC - Interstate Commerce Commission.

IN THE ROUGH - Wooden articles that are not further manufactured than sawn, hewn, planed, bent or turned.

IN THE WHITE - Wooden articles that are further manufactured than "in the rough," but including not more than one coat of priming.

inv. - Invoice

K

KD - Knocked down.

kg. - Kilogram.

KD FLAT - An article taken apart, folded or telescoped to reduce its bulk at least 66 2/3% below its assembled size.

KNOCKED DOWN (KD) - An article taken apart folded or telescoped in such a manner as to reduce its bulk at least 33 1/3% below its assembled bulk.

L

L.&D. - Loss and damage.

L.A. - Letter of authority.

L/C - Letter of credit.

L.C.L. - Less than carload.

l.c.m. - Least common multiple.

ldg. - Loading

LESS THAN TRUCKLOAD (LTL) - Rates applicable when the quantity of freight is less than the volume or truckload minimum weight.

LINER - A liner is a vessel, usually a common carrier, engaged in the carriage of general cargo along a definite route on a fixed schedule.

ltge. - Lighterage.

LTL - Less than truckload.

M

M.A. FORM - Special form of invoice required for shipment to Canada.
MDSE. - Merchandise.
MEASUREMENT TON - The measurement ton (also known as the cargo ton or freight ton) is a space measurement, usually 40 cubic feet or one cubic meter. The cargo is assessed a certain rate for every 40 cubic feet of space it occupies.
min. wt. - Minimum weight.
MW - Minimum weight factor.

N

NESTED - Three or more different sizes of an article are placed within each other so that each article will not project above the next lower article by more than 33 1/3% of its height.
NESTED SOLID - Three or more different sizes of an article are placed within each other so that each article will not project above the next lower article by more than 1/4 inch.
NMFC - National Motor Freight Classification.
N.O.E. - Not otherwise enumerated.
N.O.H.P. - Not otherwise herein provided.
N.O.I. - Not more specifically described.
N.O.I.B.N. - Not otherwise indicated by number; Not otherwise indicated by name.
N.O.S. - Not otherwise specified.
N.S.P.F. - Not specifically provided for.

O

O/A - Open account.
O/N - Order notify.
O.R. - Owners Risk.
O.S.&D. - Over, short and damage.
o.t. – On truck or railway

P

P.A. - Particular average.
P.D. - Per diem.
PLACE - A particular street address or other designation of a factory, store, warehouse, place of business, private residence, construction camp or the like, at a point (See POINT).
POINT - A particular city, town, village or other community or area which is treated as a unit for the application of rates.
PPD. - Prepaid.
PRO NUMBER - A number assigned by the carrier to a single shipment, used in all cases where the shipment must be referred to. Usually assigned at once.
P.W. - Packed weight.

R

REFG. - Refrigerating; Refrigeration.
R.I.T. - Refining in transit.
R.S. or L. - Classes the same or lower.

S

S.C. &S. - Strapped, corded and sealed.
S/D - Sight draft.
S.D.D. - Store door delivery.
sdg. - Siding
SET UP - Articles in their assembled condition.
SHIPMENT - A lot of freight tendered to a carrier by one consignor at one place at one time for delivery to one consignee at one place or one bill of lading.
S.I.T. - Stopping in transit.
SITE - A particular platform or location for loading or unloading at a place (See PLACE).
sld. - Sailed.
S.I. &C. - Shipper's load and count.
S.O. - Ship's option; Shipping order; seller's option.
S.S. - Shipside.
S/S - Steamship.
STDS. - Standards.
str. - Steamer.
S.U. - Set up.
S.U.C.I. - Set up carload.
S.U.I.C.L. - Set up in less than carload.

T

t/d/b/a - Trading and doing business as.
TL - Truckload.
t.l.o. - Total loss only.
TON - Freight rates for liner cargo generally are quoted on the basis of a certain rate per ton, depending on the nature of the commodity. This ton, however, may be a weight ton or a measurement ton.
TRAMP - A tramp ship is a vessel that does not operate along a definite route on a fixed schedule, but calls at any port where cargo is available.
TRUCKLOAD - Truckload rates apply where the tariff shows a truckload minimum weight. Charges will be at the truckload minimum weight unless weight is higher.

U

U.S.S.G. - U.S. standard guage.
u/w - Underwriter.

V

val. - Value.
VES. - Vessel.
viz. - Namely.
VOL. - Volume
VOLUME - Volume rates or classes are those for which a volume minimum weight (Vol. min. wt.) is provided; charges will be assessed at the volume minimum weight shown in the tariff except that actual weight will apply when in excess of the volume minimum weight.

W

W.&I. - Weighing and inspection.
W/B - Waybill.
w.p.a. - With particular average.